# *God Transcendent*

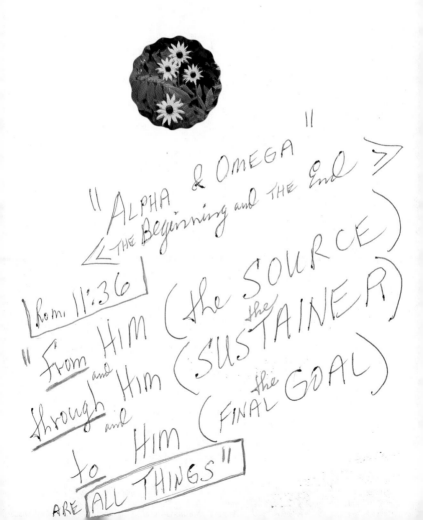

" ALPHA & OMEGA "

← THE Beginning and THE End →

[Rom. 11:36]

" From HIM (the SOURCE)

and through HIM (the SUSTAINER)

and to HIM (the FINAL GOAL)

ARE [ALL THINGS] "

# God Transcendent

J. GRESHAM MACHEN

*Edited by*
NED BERNARD STONEHOUSE

THE BANNER OF TRUTH TRUST

132041

THE BANNER OF TRUTH TRUST

*3 Murrayfield Road, Edinburgh EH12 6EL*
*P.O. Box 621, Carlisle, Pennsylvania 17013, USA*

\*

© Wm B Eerdmans Publishing Company, 1949
*First published 1949*
*First Banner of Truth edition 1982*
*ISBN 0 85151 355 7*

\*

Set in VIP Century Schoolbook

Filmset, printed and bound in Great Britain by
Hazell Watson & Viney Ltd, Aylesbury, Bucks

# Contents

# Introduction

FOR well over a decade before his untimely death on January 1st, 1937, J. Gresham Machen was recognised by many as the most valiant and eloquent spokesman for orthodox Christianity in America, if not in the entire world. Speaking on the background of many years of collaboration and intimate friendship, but also as a well-informed and keen observer of theological and ecclesiastical developments, Professor Caspar Wistar Hodge of Princeton characterised Dr Machen as being, at the time of his passing, 'the greatest theologian in the English-speaking world' and 'the greatest leader of the whole cause of evangelical Christianity.' At the same time Dr R. A. Meek, a prominent Southern Methodist, hailed him as 'the first Protestant minister in the nation' and 'the ablest exponent and defender of evangelical Christianity.' More than a decade earlier Dr John A. Hutton, influential editor of *The British Weekly*, introduced him most warmly to his readers and devoted an extended series of feature articles to the book *What Is Faith?*, which had been published in 1925. And the brilliant Religious Editor of the *Boston Evening Transcript*, Albert C. Dieffenbach, himself a Unitarian, eulogised him as being 'as learned and valiant a spiritual warrior as the Protestant Church has produced in modern times, ... a Christian of apostolic ardour,' and as one who 'sought the truth diligently, devotedly, and with dedication.'

Nor was the recognition of Dr Machen's eminence as a Christian spokesman restricted to the ecclesiastical world. Walter Lippmann, speaking of *Christianity and Liberalism*, which had been published in 1923, said: 'It is an admirable book. For its acumen, for its saliency and for its wit, this cool and stringent defence of orthodox Protestantism is, I think, the best popular argument produced by either side. We shall do well to listen to Dr Machen. The Liberals have yet to answer him.' And H. L. Mencken, himself a sceptic of the deepest dye, singled out Machen on more than one occasion for his heroic defence of Christianity in which – so Mr Mencken judged – he had every advantage, both logical and moral, over his modernist opponents.

The reputation of Professor Machen was most firmly established by the impact made by his widely read books. His trenchant *The Origin of Paul's Religion* (1921) and his masterful *The Virgin Birth of Christ* (1930; rev. edit. 1932) are monumental contributions to the exposition and defence of the Christian Faith, and constitute the chief evidences of his profound and articulate scholarship. *New Testament Greek for Beginners* (1923 *ff.*), while designed for elementary instruction, is an admirably concise and lucid textbook which could have been prepared only by a master of the subject and has proved a delight to teachers for twenty-five years. The other books from his pen, though far from superficial, soon gained and still retain a wide popular appeal. In addition to the two works mentioned in the preceding paragraphs, they include especially the volumes of radio addresses entitled *The Christian Faith in the Modern World* (1936) and *The Christian View of Man* (1937), in which he presented a fresh and effective exposition of the Christian Faith from his standpoint of whole-hearted commitment to Calvinism as constituting consistent Biblical Christianity.

However basic these books are to a true estimate of Dr Machen's significance, they do not tell the whole story. Although he was a scholar and teacher of the highest rank, and had few equals in giving perspicuous literary expression to the results of meticulous research, he was far more than a master in the academic

sphere. As a preacher and speaker on conference platforms his services were in constant demand. Moreover,
he was frequently in the public eye because of his
timely and vigorous utterances on the issues of the day.
He was one of the most colourful and controversial
figures of his time, and it is doubtful that in the
ecclesiastical world of the twenties and thirties any
religious leader was more constantly in the limelight.

It is these wider and somewhat more popular aspects
of Machen's career that are brought especially to view
in this collection of sermons and addresses. Moreover,
this volume serves the purpose of making available to
the reading public a considerable body of materials
which otherwise would not be generally accessible. A
few of the items published here have indeed become
fairly widely known due to circulation in pamphlet
form, but merit inclusion in this collection for the very
reason that they were among the most influential of his
briefer writings. Many others, however, found publication in magazines and newspapers which are not
generally available. And a large number owe their
presence to the fact that access to the files of Dr Machen
has brought to light manuscripts of sermons and other
papers which were not published by the author but
which, in many instances, were widely used in the
pulpit and on public platforms over a period of many
years.

The descriptions which follow provide more specific
information concerning the character and occasion of
the individual items.

The twenty sermons presented herein, with a few
notable exceptions, were not prepared for publication
by Dr Machen, but by the editor of this volume. Several
were printed in *The Presbyterian Guardian;* others now
appear in print for the first time. Though not intended
for publication, their value is enhanced by the consideration that they were prepared *to be preached.* And they
were preached, most of them time and again. A printed

sermon perhaps never is as effective as one that is spoken, and that is surely true of Dr Machen's sermons. Yet his preaching was so free of the orator's tricks, so simple and unaffected, that it does not share the common fate of the printed sermon when seen in cold type. For his preaching was never a shallow or hollow assembly of words. The message was not contrived to adorn the messenger; the messenger was the mere instrument to herald forth the Word of God.

Although the sermons presented may be regarded as more or less representative of Machen's preaching over a period of two or more decades, the order here is broadly speaking chronological. The first eight sermons, for example, though preached on many occasions, are known to have been delivered in the sequence given during the year in which he was Stated Supply in the First Presbyterian Church of Princeton, 1923–1924.

The two following sermons (9, 10) belong to this same period, although specific evidence is lacking that they were preached in the Princeton series of 1923–1924.

The remaining sermons are distinctive in that they were prepared for special occasions. 'The Gospel and Modern Substitutes' (11) is given substantially in the form in which it was utilised as an address before the 54th State Convention of the Y.M.C.A. held in Indiana, Pennsylvania, on April 14th, 1923, but has been edited with the help of another manuscript. It is grouped with the sermons because it was used as such on a number of occasions, and though it is hardly a typical sermon it is assuredly most original and arresting. The three following sermons have in common the fact that they were first delivered in Miller Chapel in Princeton in fulfilment of the responsibility devolving upon the professors to preach to the students once a year. The first of this group (12) was preached on March 8th, 1925. Soon thereafter thousands of copies in pamphlet form were circulated throughout the world. 'Prophets

False and True' (13) was the Chapel sermon for the following year, and upon invitation of Joseph Fort Newton, editor of *Best Sermons*, 1926, was included in that volume. 'The Good Fight of Faith' (14) was preached on March 10th, 1929, and was the last sermon delivered at Princeton, for it was in that year that Dr Machen resigned his position there. 'Constraining Love' (15) was delivered at the Second General Assembly of the Presbyterian Church of America, later known as The Orthodox Presbyterian Church, on November 12th, 1936.

The final five items in this group (16–20) were radio addresses rather than sermons, but their right to a place here will perhaps not be seriously disputed. In *The Christian Faith in the Modern World* and *The Christian View of Man* we possess the popular expositions of Christian doctrine that had been prepared for radio audiences over a period of two seasons. Dr Machen had expressed the hope of continuing the series for at least two more years and thus of rounding out a survey of Christian doctrine that might prove helpful especially to college students and classes in Bible study generally. In the midst of the third year of this radio ministry, however, he was struck down, and this hope failed of fulfilment. The five messages included here are a selection from twelve manuscripts employed for the broadcasts. Although they were prepared under terrific pressure of responsibilities of many kinds, and were left in an unpolished form, they constitute valuable additions to our knowledge of his message. 'The Creeds and Doctrinal Advance' (16) was one of the first addresses in the Fall of 1936; the final four were delivered on the final four Sundays of his life, the last being given on December 27th, only five days before his death.[1]

[1] This explains why the promise given by Machen to expound the positive biblical teaching on the Atonement (e.g. p. 206) could not be fulfilled.

Special interest attaches to the next to the last address which was devoted to 'The Active Obedience of Christ,' for it provides a most illuminating background for a telegram dictated on the last day of his life to his nurse for transmission to his colleague Professor John Murray: 'I'm so thankful for active obedience of Christ; no hope without it.' Prior to the delivery of that address on December 20th, he had been discussing this precious doctrine with Mr Murray, and now as he lay at death's door he could not but bear testimony to the confidence that, through the substitutionary atonement of Christ, he enjoyed assurance, not only of full remission of sin and its penalty, but also of being accepted as perfectly obedient and righteous because of the perfect obedience of Christ to the divine will. An exultant note of triumph through the merit of his Saviour was thus sounded forth as he was about to enter the divine presence.

Acknowledgment is hereby made to Harcourt, Brace & Co. for permission to reprint 'Prophets False and True.' (13) from the volume, *Best Sermons*, 1926, edited by Joseph Fort Newton.

I wish also to express my gratitude to Miss Margaret S. Robinson for assistance in preparing copy and to my wife and the Rev. Leslie W. Sloat for their help in reading proof.

My prayer is that this volume not only may serve to enlarge the understanding and appreciation of the heroic witness of J. Gresham Machen, but also may contribute positively to the proclamation of the gospel of Jesus Christ to which he gave his life.

Ned B. Stonehouse
March 1, 1949

# 1: *God Transcendent*

*'It is he that sitteth upon the circle of the earth, and the inhabitants thereof are as grasshoppers; that stretcheth out the heavens as a curtain, and spreadeth them out as a tent to dwell in'* (Isa. 40:22).

THE fortieth chapter of Isaiah in the King James Version is one of the noblest pieces of prose in the English language. The simplest means are employed in the production of the effect; common, homely English words are used; and some of the grandest sentences are written in words of one syllable. After the lapse of three centuries there is nothing strange or archaic in the language of this chapter; the words are those that form our common English speech in the twentieth century just as in 1611. But if the materials used are simple, the total effect is sublime. There is in this chapter a rhythm that never degenerates into metre, a combination of simplicity with grandeur, which uplifts the soul. It is quite impossible, the wondering reader will say, for prose style ever to attain heights greater than these.

The marvel is that the truly English beauty of the King James Version is attained without any of that freedom – not to say licence – in translation which modern translators pronounce necessary. The original in this version is followed with admirable closeness; paraphrase is eschewed; and yet the result is an English masterpiece. The fortieth chapter of Isaiah in the Authorised Version is a masterpiece not because it is a new work – as some of our recent alleged translations of the Bible really are – but because it has reproduced faithfully both letter and spirit of the majestic original. The author of this chapter was a true poet.

That fact may well cause the devout reader to rejoice. The central worth of the Bible does not indeed depend upon literary form; the Bible is the 'best seller' not because it is a collection of inspiring literature but because it records facts. It is valuable primarily because it records the facts about God, about the lost condition of man, and about that mighty divine act – prepared for in all the long dealings of God with His people in Old Testament times – which took place outside the walls of Jerusalem nineteen hundred years ago when the guilt of sin was washed away and a new face, for believers, was put upon the world. If the Bible does not really record facts, then its literary beauty, though it may save it from utter oblivion, will succeed only in preserving a taste for it among a few select souls; and the love and veneration of the race, which it now possesses, will certainly be destroyed. The Christian religion is no mere form of mysticism, but is founded upon a body of facts; the facts are recorded in the Bible; and if the supposed facts were not facts at all, then Christianity and the Bible would certainly sink into a common ruin.

Nevertheless, though the primary importance of the Bible is found in its recording of facts, the way in which the facts are recorded is by no means a matter of indifference. A bald, dry record of the history of redemption might possibly have convinced the mind – though even that, because of subtle moral factors involved, may be doubtful – but it would at any rate never have touched the heart. As it is, God has been very good; He has spoken to us in gracious fashion; He has condescended to persuade where He might have spoken only in a tone of cold command. He has condescended to win our hearts by the variety and beauty of His Book. In the Bible there is that which meets every need of man, which answers to every mood, which speaks to every

16

heart. No one who comes to this feast need go empty away; and there are times in every life when even the least considered of the things that the Bible contains are just what is needed by the soul. So there is a place in the nurture of the Christian life, among other things, for the majestic poetry of Isaiah.

The fortieth chapter of Isaiah was written by a prophet who revealed the truth; but the prophet was also a poet. And this poet – unlike some poets whose worth lies altogether in the music of the form and not at all in the matter – this poet had a great theme. The theme is the living God. The prophet celebrates especially the awful transcendence of God, the awful separateness between God and the world. The God of Isaiah is not the rather pathetic finite god of Mr H. G. Wells – not a god who works merely in and with striving humanity – but the sovereign King. 'It is he that sitteth upon the circle of the earth, and the inhabitants thereof are as grasshoppers.' 'Who hath directed the Spirit of the Lord, or being his counsellor hath taught him? With whom took he counsel, and who instructed him, and taught him in the path of judgment, and taught him knowledge, and shewed to him the way of understanding?' And this sovereign Person is Lord not only of mankind but also of all nature. He is very different from what modern men are accustomed to call, by a perversion of a great truth, the 'immanent' God. He pervades all, but He also transcends all, and He has never abandoned His freedom in the presence of the things that He has made. 'To whom then will ye liken me, or shall I be equal? saith the Holy One. Lift up your eyes on high, and behold who hath created these things, that bringeth out their host by number: he calleth them all by names by the greatness of his might, for that he is strong in power; not one faileth.' This is the very pinnacle of natural religion; the heavens here indeed declare the glory of God, the firmament showeth

His handiwork. The living God, according to Isaiah, is revealed through the things that He has made.

Natural religion – the revelation of God through nature – is by no means dead. Recently I listened to an interesting lecture by a famous man of science. The lecturer traced the progress of scientific investigation and pointed out, if I remember aright, its material benefits. But then he paused to speak of another product of the scientific spirit; the true scientist, he said, is brought face to face at last with the ultimate mystery and at that point he becomes a religious man. There is endless diversity in the world; but the progress of investigation has revealed the electron; and the electrons, said he, are all alike – they are machine-made. And their marvellous likeness reveals the existence of a mystery into which man cannot penetrate; in truly religious awe the man of science stands at length before a curtain that is never lifted, a mystery that rebukes all pride.

Many questions, naturally, remained as I listened in my utterly ignorant mind. I might have asked, had I been so bold, how the lecturer knew that the electrons are all alike, and if they are all alike how from them has come the endless diversity of the world. But I was sure at least that the conclusion was right. There is an ultimate mystery before which the knowledge of the wisest men is dumb. The presence of that mystery is revealed to different men in different ways. Certainly it is not obscured one whit by modern achievements, for the widening of the circle of human knowledge only increases the periphery of dreadful contact with the unknown. And even within the little circle of knowledge, mystery touches us at a thousand points. There is an aspect ever of the simplest things that is just as mysterious as those problems of electrons or quanta with which contemporary science is bold enough to deal. The modern scientist is humble and aghast in the presence of the electrons, and that is well. But Isaiah had really just as much scientific right to be humble as he contemplated in his way the starry spheres. There is nothing in modern science that has invalidated but everything that has confirmed his words: 'Lift up your eyes on high, and behold who hath created these things, that bringeth out their host by number: he calleth them all by names by the greatness of his might, for that he is strong in power; not one faileth.' Now as then the man who really thinks will stand in awe before God. We can never get away from natural religion. It is confirmed by modern science; it is confirmed and enriched by the Bible; and it is confirmed by the example of our Lord.

But is that all? The mighty prophet who wrote the words that we have read did not think that it was all. He did not content himself with standing in awe before God; but he claimed this mighty God as his. He added to the realm of nature the realm of grace. 'Who hath measured the waters in the hollow of his hand and meted out heaven with the span, and comprehended the dust of the earth in a measure, and weighed the mountains in scales, and the hills in a balance?' There is the God of mystery before whom men might well stand forever in silent fear. But that mighty ruler of the world to the prophet was also the covenant God of Israel; He was a God who had loved His people and whom His people could love. Hear what is said of this terrible God (can it be the same?)' 'He shall feed his flock like a shepherd: he shall gather the lambs with his arm, and carry them in his bosom, and shall gently lead those that are with young.' This goes far beyond all natural religion; in all the realm of nature there is little hint of this; this is revelation and revelation alone.

And can we do without it? Can we really be content with the awful mystery that nature presupposes if it does not reveal? Natural religion is indeed not to be despised. Well may lesser men emulate the example of the scientist who stands in humble awe before the dreadful curtain that veils the being of God. The awe of the true man of science is an emotion not to be despised. But can we bear to stand even before that curtain? Are we worthy even to contemplate afar that mystery that explains the world? We have offended even against nature's laws; we are unclean. Not for us the uplifting emotion of awe that is man's highest glory! We are unworthy to lift our eyes unto God, we can only grovel in the filthy sty which our baseness is making of the world.

But as we shrink in guilty fear from these high things, God has put forth His hand to draw us near. He has not concealed from us the uncleanness of our sin; He has confirmed in letters of flame the condemnation of our hearts.

But He has conquered sin and guilt by an act of love. He has come in the Person of the Son and borne our guilt: God's love has cast out fear. Isaiah had not seen the Saviour with the bodily eye; but being true prophet he saw Him with the eye of faith. There is in the Bible a grand continuity in the economy of grace. God's gracious dealings with His people of old were an anticipation of the coming of the Lord. 'Comfort ye, comfort ye my people, saith your God' – these words with which our chapter begins are fulfilled and completed in Christ.

So the dreadful curtain has been lifted. It has been lifted by a revelation which is the explanation of an act. Only a look has been granted beyond, but the look is sufficient to give life. And what is revealed in those mysterious depths beyond the veil? Something that nature could never tell. The heart of the Eternal, it is found, is most wonderfully kind. 'He shall feed his flock like a shepherd: he shall gather the lambs with his arm and carry them in his bosom, and shall gently lead those that are with young.' The gracious revelation can never destroy our sense of mystery in the presence of

God; the Lord who is our shepherd is also the dreadful ruler of all nature whose counsel none can tell. But the curtain had been drawn gently aside. But to whom has a look been granted beyond? Here is the wonder of our religion; here is the strange condescension of God. Not only to the wise and the mighty has a look been granted, not only as a reward for those who by the greatness of their knowledge and their diligence in research can lift themselves above details to philosophic contemplation of the mystery of the whole, but to plain people whom wise men despise. It is not man's way but God's way. 'I thank thee, O Father,' the Saviour said, 'Lord of heaven and earth, because thou hast hid these things from the wise and prudent, and hast revealed them unto babes. Even so, Father: for so it seemed good in thy sight.'

# 2: *Isaiah's Scorn of Idolatry*

*'He burneth part thereof in the fire; with part thereof he eateth flesh; he roasteth roast, and is satisfied: yea, he warmeth himself, and saith, Aha, I am warm, I have seen the fire: And the residue thereof he maketh a god, even his graven image; he falleth down unto it, and worshippeth it, and prayeth unto it, and saith, Deliver me; for thou art my god'* (Isa. 44:16, 17).

THIS passage expresses the scorn of the prophet for idolatry. And it would be harder to find more scathing irony in all literature. Nothing could possibly be more completely plain.

Yet even plainness such as this requires in the reader some receptiveness of soul. It might seem impossible for anyone to misunderstand; yet modern men do succeed in doing so. I remember a sermon which I heard a few years ago. It introduced those verses which voice the scorn of the ancient prophet for the man who makes an idol by cutting off a piece of a stick of wood. 'He burneth part thereof in the fire; with part thereof he eateth flesh; he roasteth roast, and is satisfied: yea, he warmeth himself and saith, Aha, I am warm, I have seen the fire: And the residue thereof he maketh a god, even his graven image; he falleth down unto it, and worshippeth it, and prayeth unto it, and saith, Deliver me; for thou art my god.' Such words, it might be thought, are plain enough; surely it is impossible to misunderstand. But what did our modern friend make of these devastating words? 'These are very useful verses,' he said in effect; 'they show that the church should satisfy the material as well as the spiritual needs of man. That artificer of whom the prophet speaks made a god out of his stick, and that is well; but he also made a fire of it and roasted meat, and that also is well. So we should emulate him; we should in our church have worship – that element is well enough if it be kept in its proper place – but we should also have material service; in worshipping the god we should not neglect the making of the fire and the roasting of the meat.'

It might seem impossible that such interpretation in this supposedly enlightened age, should actually exist; yet exist it does, and it threatens to dominate our modern religious world. Prejudice and narrow obscurantism in the false garb of freedom are everywhere at work. They have produced their garbled or Shorter Bibles – I suppose *Paradise Lost* could be reduced to banality if the words in it were chosen and combined anew to suit the modern reader – they have produced their alleged translations of the Bible which are not translations but falsifications. The Bible under such treatment is becoming a book with seven seals. When will it be rediscovered? When will men again read it as it is, with all its scathing rebuke to human pride, with all its exaltation of the living God? We cannot say when the blessed day will come. But one thing is clear – if the Word of God again were heard, there would again be an upheaval like the Reformation of the sixteenth century. Now, as at the end of the Middle Ages, the Bible is obscured by an interpretation which reverses its meaning; and now as well as then the rediscovery of the Bible would set the world free. That would be a beneficent upheaval; it would mean a grounding of the social edifice no longer upon the shifting sands of utilitarianism, but upon the rock of God's commands.

The fine scorn of Isaiah is not without interest at the present time. It is directed, indeed, against idolatry, and no one would seem to be in danger of idolatry today. But the glorious thing about the polemic of the Bible is that it is not merely negative. The Bible tears down only in order that it may build a better building upon the ruins of that which has been beneficently destroyed. So it is with this chapter. The prophet denounces idolatry not out of a mere love of denunciation, but because idolatry does despite to a positive thing that fires the prophet's soul. The prophet's scorn for what is false is a generous thing because it springs from a profound love of what is true. Idolatry is denounced because of devotion to the living God. The great underlying question of this chapter is the question whether we shall worship a god of our own making or the God by whom we have been made.

The question is very much alive today. We have not idolatry in the narrower sense, but of the making of gods there is no end. Turning from the living and true God, like Israel of old, we have preferred a god who will be content to serve our ends. We have built a fire and roasted roast, and we have promoted religion; and both operations are often on the same low utilitarian plane. Religion, men say, is a useful thing; it must be promoted in the interests of the state or in the interests of the community; God is the servant of man. Instead of seeking God first and testing our plans by His revealed will, we make our plans first and drag God in to help us carry them out. Religion ceases to be an end in itself and becomes a mere means to an end. Instead of the facts about God being the basis of religious experience, religious experience is made the basis of the supposed facts.

As I was walking through the streets of one of our large cities a year or so ago I saw, not an altar with this inscription, 'To An Unknown God,' but a church with a huge sign in front of it to the effect: 'Not A Member? Come on in and help make this a better community.' That is modern religion with a vengeance. It was an appeal not to sinners to seek salvation at the hands of God, but to persons, whose purposes are already all that they should be, to use religion as a mere means to accomplish their humanitarian ends. Many preachers

24

and laymen today are busily engaged in calling the righteous to repentance. And it is just as futile an effort now as it was when our Lord first recited it in the days of His flesh.

Men are not interested in the facts about God, but in what use they can make of their thoughts about Him. Creeds may vary, men say; but a man can make any creed effective in his life. Theology, they tell us, is a mere expression of Christian experience; it is a mere interpretation of an attitude of the human soul. At the present time we may still find it useful, men say in effect, to conceive of God as a Person; but there may come a time when some other conception may serve better the needs of men. Of course such pragmatism is really sceptical to the core; it is nothing but a dismal scepticism which instead of having the honest courage of its own negations decks itself out in the now meaningless language of devotion. But it is all in vain. God is quite useless if He exists only in idea. If a man regards the belief in a personal God as a mere interpretation of experience, useful only to this generation and destined to pass away as the forms of men's thought change, then even in this generation he no longer really believes in a personal God at all. Men say that we must not hold a static conception of religion; but, after all, facts, despite all our fine words, if they be real facts, are never subject to change. We may correct our errors; but if we have ever attained to truth the truth will remain true for millions upon millions of years. Shall we give up the search for truth? That is the real religious question of the day. Shall we content ourselves with the meaningless pastime of formulating creeds which are intended only to be useful and not to be true? Or has God spoken and revealed the truth?

We Christians think that He has. He has, it is true, revealed but a little. We are but finite creatures, and God has not destroyed us by showing us the full splendours of His being. Certainly the things that we know not are vastly greater than the things that we know. There are many questions which we can never answer. I received a letter in yesterday morning's mail from a gentleman in New York, a stranger to me, who appeals to me 'as a religious teacher' to reconcile the awful facts of earthquakes and tidal waves with an overruling Providence. And a stamped envelope is enclosed for reply! No, my friends, there are some things that God has not revealed. God has not invited us finite creatures to sit at the council table of the universe. He rules all things in accordance with His mysterious will. 'Who hath directed the Spirit of the Lord, or being his counsellor hath taught him? With whom took he counsel and who instructed him, and taught him in the path of judgment, and taught him knowledge, and shewed to him the way of understanding?'

But despite this infinity of mystery, there are some things that God has revealed; some things even with regard to the most mysterious of God's acts. We cannot explain the purpose of the earthquake and the fire; but we have been told some things about them. We have had our complacent judgments stilled. We have been told that we have no right to regard those horrors as indicating greater sin on the part of those who suffered than the sin of those who escaped; but we have been told on the other hand that we all deserved to suffer calamity ten thousand times greater than these; we have had revealed to us the full dreadfulness of sin in the presence of the holiness of God's being. And we have been told of the act of God's grace by which at infinite cost to God Himself – we have a right to utter these stupendous words – mercy was extended to us who deserve it not. Great are the mysteries that are not revealed; they should ever make us humble. But greater also, and at least sufficient, are the mysteries that have been revealed. And these mysteries should make us more humble still.

When will men see that nothing but truth can satisfy the longing of the human soul? Religious conceptions which are merely useful and not eternally true are not useful at all. But as it is, a deadly blight of pragmatism has fallen upon the world. The intellect is dethroned and intellectual decadence is rapidly setting in. Men are following the will-o'-the wisp of a practical religion which shall somehow be independent of facts; they are trying to produce a decent, moral life in this world while denying the basis of morality in the being of God. They have embarked on a vain search for an authority which is merely man-made and can therefore never command the reverence of man. The words of Hosea are fulfilled in the modern conception of God, as in the idolatry of the eighth century before Christ. Of the useful, non-existent, practical God of modern times also it may be said: 'The workman made it; therefore it is not God.'

The world is restless today. There are many voices but there is no peace. Men are feverishly saying to a god manufactured to serve the social needs of man: 'Deliver me; for thou art my god.' They are trying to produce decency without principle; they are trying to keep back the raging sea of passion with flimsy mud embankments of self-interest; they are trying to do without the stern, solid masonry of the will of God. When will the vain effort cease? Shall we continue on our wanderings? Shall we continue to stagger like drunken men? Shall we still fashion a divinity that shall serve our utilitarian ends? Shall we amuse ourselves with idols? Or shall we return unto God?

# 3: *The Fear of God*

*'And fear not them which kill the body, but are not able to kill the soul: but rather fear him which is able to destroy both soul and body in hell'* (Matt. 10:28).

THESE words were not spoken by Jonathan Edwards. They were not spoken by Cotton Mather. They were not spoken by Calvin, or Augustine, or by Paul. But these words were spoken by Jesus.

And when put together with the many other words like them in the Gospels, they demonstrate the utter falsity of the picture of Jesus which is being constructed in recent years. The other day, in one of the most popular religious books of the day, *The Reconstruction of Religion*, by Ellwood, I came upon the amazing assertion that Jesus concerned Himself but little with the thought of a life after death. In the presence of such assertions any student of history may well stand aghast. It may be that we do not make much of the doctrine of a future life, but the question whether Jesus did so is not a matter of taste but an historical question which can be answered only on the basis of an examination of the sources of historical information, which we call the Gospels. And if you want to answer the question, I recommend that you do what I have done, and simply go through a Gospel harmony, noting the passages where Jesus speaks of blessedness and woe in the future life. You may be surprised at the result; certainly you will be surprised if you have been affected in the slightest degree by the misrepresentation of Jesus which suffuses the religious literature of our time. You will discover that the thought not only of heaven but also the thought of hell runs all through the teaching of Jesus. It appears in all four of the Gospels; it appears in the sources, supposed to underlie the Gospels, which have been reconstructed, rightly or wrongly, by modern criticism. It is not an element which can be removed by any critical process, but simply suffuses the whole of Jesus' teaching and Jesus' life.

It runs through the most characteristic parables of Jesus – the solemn parables of the rich man and Lazarus; the unrighteous steward; the pounds; the talents; the wheat and the tares; the evil servant; the marriage of the King's Son; the ten virgins. It is equally prominent in the rest of Jesus' teaching. The judgment scene of the twenty-fifth chapter of Matthew is only the culmination of what is found everywhere in the Gospels. 'These shall go away into everlasting punishment: but the righteous into life eternal.' There is absolutely nothing peculiar about this passage amid the sayings of Jesus. If there ever was a religious teacher who could not be appealed to in support of a religion of this world, if there ever was a teacher who viewed the world under the aspect of eternity, it is Jesus of Nazareth.

These passages and a great mass of other passages like them are embedded everywhere in the Gospel tradition. So far as I know, even the most radical criticism has not tried to remove this element in Jesus' teaching. But it is not merely the amount of Jesus' teaching about the future life which is impressive; what is even more impressive is the character of it. It does not appear as an excrescence in the Gospels, as something which might be removed and yet leave the rest of the teaching intact. If this element were removed, what would be left? Certainly not the gospel itself, certainly not the good news of Jesus' saving work; for that is concerned with these high issues of eternal life and death. But not even the ethical teaching of Jesus would be left. There can be no greater mistake

29

than to suppose that Jesus ever separated theology from ethics, or that if you remove His theology – His beliefs about God and judgment, future woe for the wicked and future blessedness for the good – you can leave His ethical teaching intact. On the contrary, the stupendous earnestness of Jesus' ethics is rooted in the constant thought of the judgment seat of God. 'If thy right eye offend thee, pluck it out and cast it from thee; for it is profitable for thee to enter into life having one eye rather than having two eyes to be cast into the gehenna of fire.' These words are characteristic of all Jesus' teaching; the stupendous earnestness of His commands is intimately connected with the alternative of eternal weal or woe.

That alternative is used by Jesus to rouse men to fear. 'And fear not them which kill the body, but are not able to kill the soul: but rather fear him, which is able to destroy both soul and body in hell.' Luke records a similar saying of Jesus: 'And I say unto you my friends, Be not afraid of them that kill the body, and after that have no more that they can do. But I will forewarn you whom ye shall fear. Fear him, which after he hath killed hath power to cast into hell; yea, I say unto you, Fear him.' There are those who tell us that fear ought to be banished from religion; we ought, it is said, no more to hold before men's eyes the fear of hell; fear, it is said, is an ignoble thing. Those who speak in this way certainly have no right to appeal to Jesus; for Jesus certainly did employ, and insistently, the motive of fear. If you eschew altogether that motive in religion, you are in striking contradiction to Jesus. Here, as at many other points, a choice must be made between the real Jesus and much that falsely bears His name today. But which is right? Is Jesus right, or are those right who put out of their minds the fear of hell? Is fear altogether an ignoble thing? Is a man necessarily degraded by being afraid?

I think, my friends, that it depends altogether upon

30

that of which one is afraid. The words of our text, with the solemn inculcation of fear, are also a ringing denunciation of fear: the 'Fear him' is balanced by 'Fear not.' The fear of God is here made a way of overcoming the fear of man. And the heroic centuries of Christian history have provided abundant testimony to its efficaciousness. With the fear of God before their eyes, the heroes of the faith have boldly stood before kings and governors and said, 'Here I stand, I cannot do otherwise, God help me, Amen.'

It is certainly an ignoble thing to be afraid of bonds and death at the hands of men; it is certainly an ignoble thing to fear those who use power to suppress the right. Even the fear of God might be degrading. It all depends upon what manner of Being you hold God to be. If you think that God is altogether such an one as yourself, your fear of Him will be a degrading thing. If you think of Him as a capricious tyrant, envious of the creatures He has made, you will never rise above the grovelling fears of Caliban. But it is very different when you stand in the presence of the source of all the moral order of the universe; it is very different when God comes walking in the garden and you are without excuse; it is very different when you think of that dread day when puny deceptions will fall off and you stand defenceless before the righteous judgment throne. It is very different when not the sins of other people but your sins are being judged. Can we really, my friends, come before the judgment seat of God and stand fearlessly upon our rights? Can we really repeat, with Henley, the well-known words: 'Out of the night that covers me, black as the pit from pole to pole, I thank whatever gods may be for my unconquerable soul,' or this: 'It matters not how strait the gate, how charged with punishments the scroll, I am the master of my fate: I am the captain of my soul'?

Is this the way to overcome fear? Surely not. We can repeat such words only by the disguised cowardice of ignoring facts. As a matter of fact, our soul is not unconquerable; we are not masters of our fate or captains of our soul. Many a man has contemplated some foul deed at first with horror, and said, 'Am I a dog that I should do this thing?' And then has come the easy descent into the pit, the gradual weakening of the moral fibre, so that what seemed horrible yesterday seems excusable today; until at last, at some sad hour, with the memory of one's horror of sin still in the mind, a man awakes to the realization that he is already wallowing in the mire. Such is the dreadful hardening that comes from sin. Even in this life we are not masters of our fate; we are of ourselves certainly not captains of our bodies, and we are of ourselves, I fear, not even captains of our souls.

It is pitiable cowardice to try to overcome fear by ignoring facts. We do not become masters of our fate by saying that we are. And such blatancy of pride, futile as it is, is not even noble in its futility. It would be noble to rebel against a capricious tyrant, but it is not noble to rebel against the moral law of God.

Are we then forever subject to fear? Is there nought, for us sinners, but a certain fearful looking for of judgment and fiery indignation? Jesus came to tell us No! He came to deliver us from fear. He did not do so by concealing facts; He painted no false picture of a complacent God who should make a compact with sin; He encouraged no flattering illusions about the power of man. Jesus did not leave the realm of divine justice as it was, and establish in opposition to it a realm of love. But He introduced unity into the world by His redeeming work. He died not to abolish but to satisfy divine justice and reconcile us to God. In the days of His flesh He pointed forward to that act; He invited the confidence of man by the promise of what was to come. In our days we look back to what has already been done; our joy is in salvation already attained; our boasting is in the Cross.

Even the Christian must fear God. But it is another kind of fear. It is a fear rather of what might have been than of what is; it is a fear of what would come were we not in Christ. Without such fear there can be no true love; for love of the Saviour is proportioned to one's horror of that from which man has been saved. And how strong are the lives that are suffused with such a love! They are lives brave, not because the realities of life have been ignored, but because they have first been faced – lives that are founded upon the solid foundation of God's grace. May such lives be ours!

Perfect love casteth out fear. But if it be our love which casteth out fear, our love is only a response to the loving act of God. 'Herein is love, not that we loved God, but that he loved us and sent his Son to be the propitiation for our sins.' There is the culmination and the transformation of fear. 'Whosoever therefore shall confess me before men,' says Jesus, 'him will I confess also before my Father which is in heaven.'

# 4: *Sin's Wages and God's Gift*

*'For the wages of sin is death; but the free gift of God is eternal life in Christ Jesus our Lord'* (Rom. 6:23 A.R.V.).

SOME time ago I heard a sermon on this text by a preacher who has now retired. The sermon was not one that I agreed with altogether, but the beginning of it, I thought, was interesting. The preacher said that during the preceding summer he had met in a chance sort of way, on one of the steamers of the Great Lakes, a gentleman who turned out to be a man of large affairs, but a man who had little to do with the church. Incidentally the conversation turned to religious matters, and the man of business gave to the preacher the benefit of a little criticism. The criticism was perhaps not unworthy of attention. 'You preachers,' the outsider said, 'don't preach hell enough.'

Usually the criticism which is levelled at the church by men who know nothing about it is as valueless as ignorant criticism is in other spheres. But in this case I am inclined to think that the critic was right. We preachers do not preach hell enough, and we do not say enough about sin. We talk about the gospel and wonder why people are not interested in what we say. Of course they are not interested. No man is interested in a piece of good news unless he has the consciousness of needing it; no man is interested in an offer of salvation unless he knows that there is something from which he needs to be saved. It is quite useless to ask a man to adopt the Christian view of the gospel unless he first has the Christian view of sin.

But a man will never adopt the Christian view of sin

if he considers merely the sin of the world or the sins of other people. Consideration of the sins of other people is the deadliest of moral anodynes; it relieves the pain of conscience but it also destroys moral life. Many persons gloat over denunciations of that to which they are not tempted; or they even gloat over denunciations, in the case of other people, of sins which are also really theirs. King David was very severe when the prophet Nathan narrated to him his sordid tale of greed. 'As the Lord liveth,' said David, 'the man that hath done this thing shall surely die.' But Nathan was a disconcerting prophet. 'And Nathan said to David, Thou art the man.' That was for David the beginning of a real sense of his sin. So it will also be with us.

Of course it seems quite preposterous that we should be sinners. It was preposterous also for King David seated on his throne in the majesty of his royal robes. It was preposterous, but it was true. So also it is preposterous for us. It seems to be a strange notion to treat respectable people as sinners. In the case of college men, it seems particularly absurd. College men look so pleasant; it seems preposterous to connect them with the dreadful fact of sin. Some time ago I was reading, I think in a journal published in London, a review of a book that dealt with religious conditions among university men or young people. The author of the book spoke of the moral ideals of the young men of the present day as being summed up in the notion of being a good sport. The young men of the present day, it was said in effect, may not use the old terminology of guilt and retribution, but they dislike the man who does not know how to play fairly a match of lawn tennis and does not know how to take defeat like a gentleman. The remark of the reviewer, I thought, was eminently just. Surely, he said, with regard to this very common lawn tennis view of sin – surely, he said, among university men 'there are grimmer facts than these.' He was right, and we know he was right. He was right about university men in England; he was right about college men in America; and he was right about the rest of us as well. There are grimmer facts than poor lawn tennis and poor sport, regrettable though that no doubt is. There is, in general, in a thousand ugly forms, the grim fact of sin.

So when I speak of sin I am not talking to you about the sin of other people, but I am talking to you about *your* sin, and I am talking to myself about my sin. I am talking about that particular battle ground where you come to grips with the power of evil and where you meet your God.

Suppose that on that battle ground we have met defeat. What is the result? The answer of the text and the answer of the whole Bible is short and plain. 'The wages of sin,' says the Bible, 'is death.' I shall not pause just now to consider in detail what Paul means by 'death' – except just to point out this interesting fact, that if you want to find the most terrible descriptions of this eternal death you will find them not in Paul but in Jesus. It is the custom nowadays to appeal from the supposedly gloomy theology of Paul to the supposedly sunny practical philosophy of Jesus; but the strange thing is that it is Jesus, not Paul, who speaks of the outer darkness and the everlasting fire and of the sin that shall not be forgiven either in this world or in that which is to come. Paul is content in his Epistles to treat of the punishment of sin with some reserve – a reserve very impressive and very terrifying, it is true – but Jesus is more explicit. Jesus makes abundantly plain that the offender against God's law is facing something far more dreadful, to say the least, than mere annihilation would be. The teaching of Jesus has at the very centre of it the fear of God and the fear of hell. No human law without sanction is complete; a law without a penalty is an altogether worthless and pitiful thing. Are God's laws of this pitiful kind?

There are some people who seem to think that they

are. But as a matter of fact God's laws have attached to them sanctions compared with which all human penalties are as nothing.

The fact appears even in the course of this world. There is a deadly inexorableness about the laws of nature. Offend against the laws of health, and the result follows with a terrible certainty; no excuses will avail; crying and tears will count nothing; the retribution, however deferred, is sure. In the sphere of the physical life, it is certainly clear that the wages of sin is death. But many people think that the paymaster can be cheated, that after a life of sin we can present ourselves hopefully at the cashier's window and be paid in some different coin from that which we have earned. Do you really agree with them? Do you really think that in this accounting you can cheat? Do you really think that by care in the physical sphere you can avoid the consequences of sin? There is something within us that tells us that such is not the case; there is something within us that reveals the abyss over which we are standing, that brushes aside our petty excuses, that reveals in the inner, moral sphere, as in the physical realm, the same terrible inexorableness of law. God grant that we may not deceive ourselves! God grant that we may not hope to cheat! God grant that we may learn in time that the wages of sin is death!

There is a definiteness and certainty about wages. Wages are different from a spontaneous gift; wages, unlike a gift, are fixed. A man has done his week's work; he presents himself at the paymaster's desk, and is paid off; the matter is not discussed; the employee does not try then to strike a bargain with the cashier. The amount of the payment has been determined beforehand, and the payment itself is a purely formal, impersonal affair. So it is, somewhat, with the wages of sin. The wages have been fixed already. I do not mean that all sins are punished alike; no doubt at God's judgment seat there is a delicacy of discrimination

37

quite impossible under human laws. And I do not mean that the penalty of sin follows merely by a natural law that is independent of God. But however the law has been established, it is, when once established, inexorable. It is quite useless for a man to argue about the penalty of his sin; it is useless in the physical sphere of the laws of health, and it will be useless when we appear at last before Him who knows the secrets of the heart. Let us not deceive ourselves, my friends. The moral constitution of the universe is a very terrible thing. Let us not think that we can trifle with it. The world is governed by inexorable law. And that law establishes by an immutable decree the dreadful consequences of sin. The wages of sin is death.

At that point some preachers stop. Here stopped, for example, the noted preacher whose sermon gave us our text and our subject today. The terribleness of sin and the inexorableness of law – it is writ large in the physical organism of man and in the whole course of nature. It is also writ large in the Bible. But the Bible, unlike nature, does not stop here. 'The wages of sin is death' – it is a great truth, but it is not the end of our text. The wages of sin is death – that is the law. But the Bible contains more than the law; it contains also the gospel. 'The wages of sin is death, but the free gift of God is eternal life in Christ Jesus our Lord.'

The free gift is contrasted with wages. Yet men persist in dragging it down to the wage level; they persist in trying to make the gift of God a product of some law. They persist in regarding salvation as proceeding by some natural process from faith or from some other quality of men. They regard Christianity as founded upon permanent principles of religion instead of being founded upon an unexpected piece of news. When will the vain effort be abandoned? Salvation is nothing, or it is a free gift; it is not a principle that has been discovered but an event that has happened.

The trouble is that we are unwilling to take God at

His word. We persist in endeavouring to save ourselves. If we have learned to any degree that lesson of the law, if we have come to have a horror of sin, we persist in thinking that it depends upon us to get rid of it. We try to make use of our own moral resources in this struggle, and we fall yet deeper and deeper into the mire. When shall we take God at His word? When shall we simply accept, in faith, the gift of salvation which He has offered?

It is certainly worth accepting. It consists in 'eternal life.' We need not now ask in detail what that means. But certainly it is as glorious as the 'death' with which it is contrasted is terrible. It is certainly happiness as contrasted with woe, but it is far more than happiness. It involves service, and it involves the presence of God.

The free gift of God is an absolutely unaccountable event in the life of every man who accepts it. It is not the natural working out of a principle, but it is a thing that happens. But that happening in the soul is the result of a happening in the sphere of external history. The free gift of God is eternal life *in Christ Jesus our Lord*. There we have the central characteristic of our religion; the central characteristic of Christianity is that it is not founded merely upon what always was true but primarily upon something that happened – something that took place near Jerusalem at a definite time in the world's history. In other words, it is founded not merely upon permanent truths of religion, but upon a 'gospel,' a piece of news.

The Christian preacher, be he ever so humble, is entrusted with that gospel. We could not hope to be listened to if we had merely our own thoughts; there are so many others in the world wiser and more learned than we. But in a time of peril in a beleaguered city the humblest of day-labourers is more worth listening to than the greatest of orators, if he has news. So it is with the Christian preacher in this deadly peril of the soul. The wages of sin is death – that is the law. But at the decisive point Christ has taken the wages upon Himself – that is the gospel. Inexorable is the moral law of God. But God's mercy has used, and triumphed over, His law. We deserved eternal death; but Christ died instead of us on the cross. Shall we accept the gift? The result will be a fresh start in God's favour and then a winning battle against sin. 'The wages of sin is death; but the free gift of God is eternal life in Christ Jesus our Lord.'

# 5: *The Issue in the Church*

'*Wherefore if any man is in Christ, he is a new creature: the old things are passed away; behold, they are become new*' (2 Cor. 5:17 A.R.V.).

THE world of today is hoping for something new. Things that seemed to be new have proved to be old; the newness of modern inventions has been found not to touch the depths of life. New situations, it has been discovered, do not make new men; a man is not made over by ascending in an airplane to the sky. Novelty has been sought in every sphere, but it is not so easy to find; rebellion against accepted forms does not produce a new style, but sometimes only reveals a pitiful lack of invention; sensationalism has proved to be rather dull.

In the epistles of Paul one finds that joyous freshness which modern men are seeking in vain; the first Christians evidently were in possession of something really new. The conditions of life, it is true, were not greatly changed; social institutions in the early church were left very much as they were before. But beneath outward sameness there was a mighty inner change. The novelty of the early church was very different from the novelty of today. Today we have changing circumstances and humanity itself in a rut; then there was outward sameness, but underneath it there were new men. 'Wherefore if any man is in Christ, he is a new creature: the old things are passed away; behold, they are become new.'

Many earnest men today are examining the future with some dread. Is humanity condemned to a hopeless dulness, or may there be even now a fresh start? A fresh start is certainly not easy to achieve. It cannot be achieved simply by taking things as they come; it cannot be achieved simply by tearing off the last leaf for this year and putting a fresh calendar on the wall. The new year may prove to be old before his time. How shall next year be made really different from this: how shall the new year be made really new?

We have a startling suggestion to make. How would it be if there should be a revival of the Christian religion? At that point, no doubt – to use a figure of Mr Sunday – many of our hearers will begin to snap their watches at us; if we have no more novel suggestion than that, we shall probably find our audiences dwindling away. But the suggestion is not really so hackneyed as it seems; amid the many elixirs that are on the market today, it is astonishing how little attention is being given to the gospel of Christ. Many modern men are like a contemporary British author of whom it has been said that he had sympathy for every religious institution on earth except one; he has the warmest sympathy for every pagan religion no matter how strange, but the Wednesday night prayer meeting he simply cannot stand. It was once remarked about a great encyclopaedia how strange it was that the principle of that work, in accordance with which various types of religious belief were to be presented by their own adherents, was not applied to evangelical Christianity, at least in its consistent form. Other beliefs are presented in the great encyclopaedia by their friends; evangelical Christianity alone (at least in the form of the Reformed Theology) is presented by its opponents. The same unfairness prevails in many circles today. Various religious beliefs are given a hearing, but this tolerance is not allowed to extend to the gospel of the cross of Christ. The discrimination may perhaps be excused by the incorrigibly insistent character of the gospel appeal, but it should not be excused on improper grounds. It should not be excused on the ground of breadth or tolerance. The prevailing attitude towards evangelical Christianity may be necessary in order to avoid trouble; it may be safe and prudent: but tolerant, at any rate, it certainly is not.

The prejudice against Christianity may ultimately become beneficial. It may be that when the Wednesday night prayer meeting becomes as strange as dervish dances it will be revived as a great new discovery to which the attention of men will turn. Already there is the most abysmal ignorance of the gospel; the Epistle to the Galatians, even among scholars, is almost as much a sealed book as it was just before Luther's day. Yet it is really so gloriously plain. When will it be rediscovered?

When it is rediscovered there will be great revival of the Christian religion. None can say how soon that will come, and certainly it will not be produced by human effort. It will come not by might and not by power, but by the Spirit of the Lord of Hosts. Yet although a revival of the Christian religion is not the product of human effort, there are certain favourable conditions which the Spirit may first produce and then use for the accomplishment of His beneficent work.

Those favourable conditions fall into two classes. First, there are those conditions which may be expected to appeal to all men, whether Christians or not, provided only they are really seeking some spiritual advance; in the second place, there are those conditions which will be appreciated by Christians alone.

Under the former head may be mentioned tolerance or religious liberty – the freedom of any citizens to hold, propagate, and teach to their children any form of religious belief that they desire. Tolerance was a great achievement for our forefathers. But now, apparently, in America, it is being given up. It has been given up, for example, in Oregon, where a law soon to go into effect requires that all children up to sixteen years of age (until a certain grade has been reached) shall

43

attend the public schools. Private schools and Christian schools are thus legislated out of existence, and children are taken forcibly from their parents and placed under the despotic control of whatever superintendent of education happens to be in office in the district where they reside. Similar legislation has been proposed in many other states, and the dangerous Towner-Sterling bill in Congress has as its ultimate tendency (whatever temporary safeguards there may be) the establishment of a uniformity of education which is the most appalling calamity into which any nation could fall. It would be difficult to imagine, at any rate, a worse tyranny than that of the Oregon type. Place children in their formative years under the despotic control of experts appointed by the state, and you have a really more effective interference with civil and religious liberty than the Inquisition, perhaps, ever achieved. It is true that hopeful signs are not altogether absent. The abominable Lusk Laws in the State of New York, though by the scantiest majority, were repealed; and the decision written by Justice McReynolds, of the United States Supreme Court, concerning the Nebraska language law (which practically made literary education a crime) shows that the principles of American liberty are not yet entirely dead. But the danger is certainly very great. Unless there is tolerance on the part of the state, any great spiritual advance, whatever its direction may be thought to be, will be hindered. It will not, I suppose, be prevented. Men of real convictions now as always may perhaps maintain their convictions even under a hostile government. But why should the old battle for freedom be fought again? Why should we not retain the freedom which, at such great cost, our fathers won?

The second of the general conditions favourable to any spiritual advance is honesty – just plain old-fashioned honesty of speech. That condition in certain religious circles is largely absent today. Traditional terminology is constantly being used in a double sense. Plain people in the church are being told, for example, that this preacher or that believes that Jesus is God. They go away much impressed; the preacher, they say, believes in the deity of Christ; what more could be desired? What is not being told them is that the word 'God' is being used in a pantheising or Ritschlian sense, so that the assertion, 'Jesus is God,' is not the most Christian, but the least Christian thing that the modernist preacher says. The modernist preacher affirms the deity of Jesus not because he thinks high of Jesus but because he thinks desperately low of God.

Formerly when men had brought to their attention perfectly plain documents like the Apostles' Creed or the Westminster Confession or the New Testament, they either accepted them or else denied them. Now they no longer deny, but merely 'interpret.' Every generation, it is said, must interpret the Bible or the creed in its own way. But I sometimes wonder just how far this business of interpretation will go. I am, let us say, in a company of modern men. They begin to test my intelligence. And first they test me on the subject of mathematics. 'What does six times nine make?' I am asked. I breathe a sigh of relief; many questions might place me very low in the scale of intelligence, but that question I think I can answer. I raise my hand hopefully. 'I know that one,' I say. 'Six nines are fifty-four.' But my complacency is short-lived. My modern examiner puts on a grave look. 'Where have you been living?' he says. ' "Six nines are fifty-four" – that is the old answer to the question.' In my ignorance I am somewhat surprised. 'Why,' I say, 'everybody knows that. That stands in the multiplication table; do you not accept the multiplication table?' 'Oh, yes,' says my modern friend, 'of course I accept the multiplication table. But then I do not take a static view of the multiplication table; every generation must interpret the multiplication table in its own way. And so of course I accept the proposition that six nines are fifty-four, but I interpret that to mean that six nines are a hundred and twenty-eight.' And then the examination gets into the sphere of history. The examiner asks me where the Declaration of Independence was adopted. That one, also, I think I know. 'The Declaration of Independence,' I say, 'was adopted at Philadelphia.' But again I meet with a swift rebuke. 'That is the old answer to the question,' I am told. 'But,' I say, 'everyone knows that the Declaration of Independence was adopted at Philadelphia; that stands in all the history books; do you not accept what stands in the history books?' 'Oh, yes,' says my modern friend, 'we accept everything that stands in the history books – hundred per cent Americans we are. But then, you see, we have to interpret the history books in our own way. And so of course we accept the proposition that the Declaration of Independence was adopted at Philadelphia, but we interpret that to mean that it was adopted at San Francisco.' And then finally the examination turns (though still in the sphere of history) to the department of history that concerns the Christian religion. 'What do you think happened,' I am asked, 'after Jesus was laid in that tomb near Jerusalem about nineteen hundred years ago?' To that question also I have a very definite answer. 'I will tell you what I think happened,' I say; 'He was laid in the tomb, and then the third day He arose again from the dead.' At this point the surprise of my modern friend reaches its height. The idea of a professor in a theological seminary actually believing that the body of a dead man really emerged from the grave! 'Everyone,' he tells me, 'has abandoned that answer to the question long ago.' 'But,' I say, 'my friend, this is very serious; that answer stands in the Apostles' Creed as well as at the centre of the New Testament; do you not accept the Apostles' Creed?' 'Oh, yes,' says my modern friend, 'of course I accept the Apostles' Creed; do we not say it every Sunday in church? – or, if we do not say it, we sing it –

of course, I accept the Apostles' Creed. But then, do you not see, every generation has a right to interpret the creed in its own way. And so now of course we accept the proposition that "the third day He arose again from the dead," but we interpret that to mean, "The third day He did *not* rise again from the dead." '

In view of this modern art of 'interpretation,' one may almost wonder whether the lofty human gift of speech has not become entirely useless. If everything that I say can be 'interpreted' to mean its exact opposite, what is the use of saying anything at all? I do not know when the great revival of religion will come. But one thing is perfectly clear. When it does come, the whole elaborate art of 'interpretation' will be brushed aside, and there will be a return, as there was at the Reformation of the sixteenth century, to plain common sense and common honesty.

Such are the general conditions of any great spiritual advance – the conditions which may be expected to appeal to friends and foes of Christianity alike. The latter condition, in particular, is not a matter that concerns merely specifically Christian ethics; outsiders can get the point as well as we. *The Freeman*, of New York, can hardly be accused of being a 'fundamentalist' organ. Yet in a recent issue I read the following very sensible words:

> We cannot help wondering why some of the clergy and laity who are being denounced by the 'fundamentalists' should appear so anxious to parry the accusation of heresy which their opponents urge against them. Heretics they certainly are, whether the standard of judgment be a formal creed to which they have subscribed or the time-honoured views of Christian faith and practice with which they are assumed, quite justly, to be in agreement. Whatever else Christianity may or may not be, it is surely not a scheme of salvation by indirection and avoidance; why, then, try to dodge the issue? Men do not, apparently, very much hesitate to call themselves heretics in politics or

education or literature or conventional morals; and a goodly number may be found who have broken openly with their old associations, and as openly gone about forming new ones; why not welcome the charge of heresy in religion and bear it as a mark of spiritual and intellectual courage, as it once was borne? There might be some martyrs, and martyrdom, we dare say, is disagreeable; but even that fate would be more honourable than the attempt to argue the words out of an instrument, or the seal off a bond.

To that in the main I can certainly subscribe. Only I do not believe that the martyrdom, which is the price of honesty, will be very serious. It must never be forgotten that in this issue in the church we are dealing with purely voluntary organisations; and we are dealing (in the Presbyterian Church at least) with the requirements, not for the church membership, but for the holding of office. No man is required to enter the ministry of the Presbyterian Church. If he is not in agreement with the faith for the propagation of which the church (in accordance with its constitution) plainly exists, he can enter into some other organization of his own. And in doing so he will have the world very largely with him. There will be some obvious disadvantages, but they will be overbalanced by the advantage of honesty. The full personal respect, even of opponents, will be regained, and the whole discussion will be lifted to a loftier plane.

Tolerance on the part of the state, and its corollary, the right of individuals to associate themselves for the propagation of any creed which they may honestly hold, no matter how foolish it may seem to others – these are the general conditions of any spiritual advance.

But for a revival of the Christian religion, the Christian man knows that there are other and more specific conditions. With them we have now hardly time to deal. But it is hoped that every function of the church may serve in some sort to impress them on the worshippers' minds. One thing now needs to be said. In leaving the way open for a revival of the Christian religion we ought not to set up false antitheses; we ought not to say, as many are saying, that instead of controversy we favour prayer. As a matter of fact, what is needed is not prayer alone and not controversy alone, but prayer and controversy both – a controversy in which a Christian is impelled to engage when he rises from his knees. Indeed, in these days, true Christian prayer is quite impossible without bold witnessing for the truth. Never was it more abundantly plain that our Lord came not to bring peace, but a sword. It is quite useless to do what many are doing; it is quite useless to read the thirteenth chapter of First Corinthians, while, at the same time, in the face of opposition we are ashamed of Christ. The plain fact is, disguised though it be by the use of traditional language, that two mutually exclusive religions are contending for the control of the church today. One is the great redemptive religion known as Christianity; the other is the naturalistic or agnostic Modernism, essentially the same, I suppose, as the religion of the Positivists or of Professor Ellwood, which is opposed, not at one point, but at every point, to the Christian faith. A separation between the two is the crying need of the hour; that separation alone can bring Christian unity. That does not mean that we are without sympathy for those who differ from us with regard to this great concern of the soul; on the contrary, many of us, in the years of struggle, have faced only too clearly the possibility that we, too, might be forced to go with the current of the age and relinquish the Christian faith. We are certainly not without admiration for the many high qualities of that type of thought and life which the non-doctrinal religion of the present day, at its best, is able to show. But we are also not without admiration for Socrates and Plato; yet Christian they certainly were not. Christianity is a peculiar type of life which is founded upon a distinctive message;

and where it loses its sense of its separateness it ceases to exist.

Christian prayer and Christian piety, we believe, are based only upon faithfulness to the Christian message and to Him who is the substance of it. We are grieved, therefore, when those who in the councils of the church have just (though we hope unwittingly) denied their Lord, think that they have made all well by reading the thirteenth chapter of First Corinthians before the assembled church. The apostle who wrote that chapter would have been surprised indeed to discover that Christian love is being set in opposition to 'the truth of the gospel.' Very different is the deeper love that is only a response to the love of God in the cross of Jesus Christ.

But it ought never to be forgotten that the author of any true revival is the Spirit of God. We ought to welcome certain conditions – we ought to welcome, I think, the controversy which has at least destroyed our complacency and turned our minds from trivialities to consider the foundations of our faith. We ought to carry on the controversy without thought of personal advantage and without the desire to get the better of an opponent in an argument. If we are animated by low motives, God will hardly honour our witness; but, on the other hand, He will not honour a witness that is false, no matter how high the motives of it may be. We certainly ought to carry on the controversy in love – love, even for those who are opponents with regard to this great concern of the soul. We certainly cannot, it is true, without hypocrisy and unfaithfulness, pray *with* those who are adherents of a different religion from ours, whether they be in the visible church or outside of it; power does not come when we bow in the house of Rimmon. But though we cannot pray with our opponents, we certainly ought to pray *for* them with all our hearts. But it is all, in itself, without avail. God Himself must determine when the gospel will again be brought to light. And who can say how soon He will put forth

His power to save? The gospel of the cross displays a wonderful power of recuperation. It seems sometimes to be buried forever, as in the religion of the Middle Ages, but then it bursts forth anew and sets the world aflame.

At present we are inarticulate; we know the riches of the gospel; we wonder at those who have it already at hand and yet are content instead with the weak and beggarly elements. When will God raise up the man of His choice to give His message powerfully to the world? We cannot say. But the truth is not dead, and God has not deserted His church. Behind all the darkness and perplexity of the present time we can discern, on the basis of the promises of God, the dawn of a better day. There may come a time, sooner than we can tell, when again we can cry in the church, as every redeemed soul cries even now: 'The old things are passed away; behold they are become new.'

# 6: *The Letter and the Spirit*

*'The letter killeth, but the Spirit giveth life'* (2 Cor. 3:6)

THIS is perhaps the most frequently misused utterance in the Bible. It is true, it has in this respect much competition. Many phrases in the New Testament are being used today to mean almost their exact opposite, as for example when the words, 'God in Christ,' and the like, are made to be the expression of the vague pantheism so popular just now, or as when the entire gospel of redemption is regarded as a mere symbol of an optimistic view of man against which that doctrine was in reality a stupendous protest. One is reminded constantly at the present time of the way in which the Gnostics of the second century used Pauline texts to support their thoroughly un-Pauline systems. The historical method of study, in America at least, is very generally being abandoned; and the New Testament writers are being made to say anything that twentieth-century readers could have wished to say.

This abandonment of scientific historical method, which appears in particularly crass form in Professor Goodspeed's translation of the great Pauline passages regarding justification, is a peculiar phenomenon, since it is practised just by those who are most contemptuous of anything that smacks of the past. If there is anything in which modern scholarship has prided itself, it is the method of interpretation which distinguishes sharply what we should have said from what an ancient writer actually did say. Like other things which modern men delight to honour, that method has a long name applied to it – it is called 'grammatico-historical exegesis.' That is a long name for a very simple thing; it simply means that, in interpreting an ancient author, we ought to divest ourselves so far as possible of our own habits of thought and look upon the world for a moment with the ancient author's eyes. The question whether, after we have done that, we shall accept as true what the ancient author says is quite a distinct question. And so when it comes to Paul, there have been many excellent expositions of his letters by men who hardly believe a word of what he says. There are two ways of being a good interpreter of Paul: one way is to be yourself in sympathy with Paul and hold the same opinions as his; the other way is to care so little about his teaching for yourself that you are able to present it as it is without testing it by your own likes or dislikes. But the attempt to find in Paul a type of religion diametrically opposite to his is of course the ruin of exegesis. So it is when Paul is being treated as though he were an adherent of that non-redemptive, optimistic religion of humanity which is so popular today.

'The letter killeth, but the Spirit giveth life' – these words are constantly being used to justify all kinds of crassly un-Pauline notions. They are being interpreted, in particular, as indicating that Paul took the law of God with a grain of salt, or as though he meant that the Old Testament were not true throughout, but that one should get just the general religious teaching of it and be content with that. Such an interpretation involves a complete abandonment of historical method. Do not think that the rejection of it is any mark of 'conservatism' in theology or the like; the great radicals are fully agreed with us in their representation of Paul's attitude towards the truth of the Scriptures. They hold that Paul accepted the Scriptures as true, though they believe that he was wrong in doing so; we hold that he accepted the Scriptures as true and was right in doing so: but both of us are fully agreed in holding that Paul did accept the Scriptures as true. We differ about the value of his teaching; but we agree at this point about what his teaching was.

Paul is not in this verse contrasting the spirit of the law with the letter of the law; he certainly does not mean that the law of Moses was not literally valid. On the contrary, he plainly believed that the ceremonial requirements of the law were just as divine as what we should call the 'moral' requirements; they were commands which God issued to His people and which His people were required to obey. Only, Paul believed that those ceremonial commands were intended by God to be temporary; they were intended to be preparatory to the coming of Christ.

It does not follow that, because a command was later abrogated or supplemented by God, therefore it had never been a command of God at all. If your father tells you to chop up the wood that is in the woodpile, that does not mean that you are to continue to chop wood to the end of time. You are not disobeying your father if you quit when the job is done. So God commanded His people to be separate from other nations. In New Testament times that middle wall of partition was broken down. But that did not mean that the previous command had not under the old dispensation been valid. The truth is that the historic and progressive character of God's command is at this point ignored just by those who make most of the idea of progress.

Jesus and His apostles were conscious of standing at the threshold of a new age – a new age which was to be ushered in, or had been ushered in, by an event. If they regarded requirements of the ceremonial law as no longer valid, or if they supplemented even the 'moral' law, as it is set forth in the Old Testament, by higher commands, that means not that they recognized a general right of man as man to take God's law with a grain of salt, but that they had a tremendous consciousness of special divine authority as those who were to usher in a new dispensation of God. When Jesus contrasted with what had been said to men of old time His own tremendous 'But I say unto you,' that does not mean at all that He held a modern low view of the truth of the Old Testament Scripture or a modern subjective notion of law as merely imposed for convenience by man upon himself; but it involves a tremendous assertion of His own unique divine authority – His authority to change what had been intended for one dispensation into what was intended for another. Jesus claimed the right to legislate for the kingdom of God. But that claim is altogether misunderstood and vilified if it is extended to man as man. In reality it involves not a mere assertion of the rights of man as man but a stupendous assertion of Jesus' rights as the Son of God. And so it is also with the authority of the apostles. That authority did not belong to them, as Jesus' authority had belonged to Him, in their own right; they could never have set over against God's law, any 'But I say unto you' of their own, as Jesus had done. But they did possess an authority delegated to them by Jesus, and in the plenitude of that apostolic authority they wrote.

Thus if Paul for his converts rejected circumcision and the ceremonial law, that does not mean at all that he was merely following the 'spirit' of the Old Testament law as distinguished from its 'letter' – the distinction is modern and un-Pauline – but it means that the great redeeming act of Christ's death to which the old dispensation had been preparatory and toward which the ceremonial law had looked – that that great act according to Paul had now been accomplished and a new and higher dispensation had been ushered in. The period of childhood was over, and the period of evangelical freedom had come.

But in our verse, Paul is not thinking specially of the ceremonial law at all. The law of which he speaks is the whole law of God, and he is thinking of it specially in its highest moral aspects in which it is valid beyond the end of time. The contrast between the letter and

55

Spirit is not a contrast between one aspect of the law and another aspect, but it is a contrast between the whole law of God on the one side and something that is not law at all on the other. Paul is not contrasting the letter of law with the spirit of the law, but he is contrasting the law of God with the Spirit of God.

The law, Paul means, is, as law, external; it is God's holy will to which we must conform. But it contains in itself no promise of its fulfilment; it is one thing to have the law written, and quite another thing to have it obeyed; in fact, because of the sinfulness of our hearts, because of the power of the flesh, the recognition of God's law only makes sin take on the definite form of transgression, it only makes sin more exceeding sinful. The law of God was written on tables of stone or on the rolls of the Old Testament books, but it was quite a different thing to get it written in the hearts and lives of the people.

So it is today. The text is of very wide application. The law of God is 'letter': it is a thing written external to the hearts and lives of men. It is written in the Old Testament; it is written in the Sermon on the Mount; it is written in the stupendous command of love for God and one's neighbour; it is written in whatever way we become conscious of the commands of God. Do not think that such an extension of the text involves the anti-historical modernising which we have just denounced; on the contrary it is amply justified by the Epistles of Paul themselves. 'When the Gentiles,' Paul says, 'which have not the law, do by nature the things contained in the law, these, having not the law, are a law unto themselves' (Rom. 2:14). The Old Testament law is just a clear, authentic expression of a law of God under which all men stand.

And that law, according to Paul, issues a dreadful, majestic sentence of eternal death. 'The soul that sinneth it shall die.' Not the hearer of the law is justified, but the doer of it. And alas, none are doers;

all have sinned. The law of God is holy and just and good; it is inexorable, and we have fallen under its just condemnation.

That is at bottom what Paul means by 'The letter killeth.' He does not mean that attention to pedantic details shrivels and deadens the soul. No doubt that is true, within certain spheres; it is a useful thought. But it is trivial indeed compared with what Paul means. Something far more majestic, far more terrible, is meant by the Pauline phrase. The letter that Paul means is the dreadful handwriting of ordinances that was against us, and the death with which it kills is the eternal death of those who are forever separated from God.

But that is not all of the text. The letter killeth, Paul says, but the Spirit maketh alive. There is no doubt about what he means by 'the Spirit.' He does not mean the spirit of the law as contrasted with the letter; he certainly does not mean the lax interpretation of God's commands which is dictated by human lust or pride; he certainly does not mean the spirit of man. No real student of Paul has doubted, so far as I know, but that he means the Spirit of God. God's law brings eternal death because of sin; but God's Spirit, shed abroad in the heart, brings life. The thing that is written killeth, but the Holy Spirit in the heart gives life.

The contrast runs all through the New Testament. Hopelessness under the law is described in the seventh chapter of Romans. 'Oh wretched man that I am! who shall deliver me from the body of this death?' But this hopelessness is transcended by the gospel. 'I thank God through Jesus Christ our Lord... For the law of the Spirit of life in Jesus Christ hath made me free from the law of sin and death.' The law's sentence of condemnation was borne for us by Christ who suffered in our stead; the handwriting of ordinances which was against us – the dreadful 'letter' of which Paul speaks in our text – was nailed to the cross. We have a fresh start in the path of God. And the Spirit of God enters into our hearts in the work of God's grace. The New Testament deals with this work gloriously from beginning to end. This giving of life of which Paul speaks in our text, is the new birth, the new creation; it is Christ who liveth in us. Here is the fulfilment of the great prophecy of Jeremiah: 'But this shall be the covenant that I will make with the house of Israel; after those days, saith the Lord, I will put my law in their inward parts, and write it in their hearts' (Jer. 31:33). The law is no longer for the Christian a command which it is for him by his own strength to obey, but its requirements are fulfilled through the mighty power of the Holy Spirit. There is the glorious freedom of the gospel. The gospel does not abrogate God's law, but it makes men love it with all their hearts.

How is it with you, my friends? The law of God stands over against you; you have offended against it in thought, word and deed; its majestic 'letter' pronounces a sentence of death against your sin. Will you attain a specious security by ignoring God's law, and by taking refuge in an easy law of your own devising? Or shall the Lord Jesus as He is offered to you in the gospel wipe out the sentence of condemnation that was against you, and shall the Holy Spirit write God's law in your heart, and make you a doer of the law and not a hearer only? So, and so only, will the text be applied to you: 'The letter killeth, but the Spirit giveth life.'

# 7: *The Brotherhood in Christ*

*'For ye are all sons of God, through faith, in Christ Jesus. For*
*as many of you as were baptised into Christ did put on Christ.*
*There can be neither Jew nor Greek, there can be neither bond*
*nor free, there can be no male and female; for ye are all one*
*man in Christ Jesus'* (Gal. 3:26–28 A.R.V.)

WHAT are the really great moments of history? Our first
impulse, in answering this question, might be to enu-
merate the great battles, the days when cities were
captured or empires won. But it is doubtful whether we
should be correct. There are other events even more
important than these. The really great moments of
history are the moments which mark the first enunci-
ation of great ideas. Ideas, after all, are the great
conquerors; they cross the best-dug trenches; they cut
the most intricate barbed wire; they move armies like
puppets; they build empires and pull them down.

So this great utterance of Paul contains in small
compass much of the subsequent history of the human
race. 'There can be neither Jew nor Greek, there can be
neither bond nor free, there can be no male and female'
– what an immense driving force has been exerted by
these truly pregnant words! The idea of a human
brotherhood in comparison with which the distinctions
of social condition, of race, and even the distinction
between the sexes would sink into insignificance – what
a great moment it was when this idea was first given
classical expression by the Apostle Paul! We are not
ashamed to say so even at the present day – even at a
time when racial hatred runs high and the opposition
of class to class, everywhere at work, has in some

places, as in Russia broken forth in orgies of blood. The words of Paul have certainly not come to full fruition; but forgotten they have never been even in the darkest and most warlike hours. They have not conquered the world, but at least they have not left the world at rest. And without them mankind would be in despair. We live in the midst of hatred and war and rumours of war but amid all the confusion of the age we comfort ourselves with the hope of the time when 'there can be neither Jew nor Greek, there can be neither bond nor free.'

The ideal of a universal human brotherhood is one of the underlying forces in the life of men. And that ideal is indissolubly connected with the Christian religion. But why is it that the ideal is so far from realisation; why is it that there has seemed rather to be a terrible retrogression from it in the past few years? Perhaps the reason may be that the Christian idea has been misunderstood and another idea substituted for it. True Christianity has power; but perhaps it may turn out that what men call the Christian idea of the brotherhood of man is not Christian at all.

Certainly the idea of the brotherhood of man is not in itself specifically or exclusively Christian. The Stoics of the time of Paul had apparently risen to the height of such an idea. The slaves, regarded by Aristotle as chattels, had come to be regarded, by a few noble souls, as members of a great human family. It was the noble conception of the brotherhood of man as man.

But was the Christian conception the same as this? It is often assumed to have been the same; it is often assumed that Christianity involved the discovery of an already existent human brotherhood. And there is an element of truth in the assumption. Our Lord did teach that every man, whether Jew or Gentile – and by implication, whether Christian or non-Christian – is our neighbour if he be in need. The apostles acted on the principle. The Apostle Paul, for example, had an intense passion for helping just especially those who had not been won to Christ. Nevertheless the conception of Christianity as consisting in the rediscovery of a universal and already existing human brotherhood misses the true centre of the Christian gospel. Christianity did indeed reaffirm the element of truth in the idea of the brotherhood of man; but the significant thing is that the reaffirmation is at best a mere starting point and not the substance of Christian teaching. I do not believe that in the whole New Testament you will find the word 'brother' once used to designate the relation in which man stands to man as man; in the New Testament the word 'brother' is used to mean not 'fellow-man' but 'fellow-Christian'. The Christian religion reaffirms, indeed, the truth in the Stoic idea of a universal human brotherhood; on one occasion Paul quoted a Stoic poet in support of the solidarity of the human race: 'For in him we live, and move, and have our being; as certain even of your own poets have said, For we are also his offspring.' Such things are important; the universal relation in which all men stand to one another because they have all been created by the one God – that is implied in everything that the Bible says. But though it is the necessary presupposition of the gospel, it is not the gospel itself. Christianity reaffirms the universal brotherhood of man, but it is Christianity because it proclaims a far tenderer and more intimate brotherhood of those who are in Christ.

Let us consider for a moment or two that brotherhood as it is set forth in our text.

In the first place, this Christian brotherhood is produced not by a mere direct relation between its members, but primarily by a common relation in which they all stand towards God. 'For ye are all sons of God,' says Paul. That is one point at which we often diverge nowadays from the New Testament. We are now inclined to make man the centre of our thoughts; in the New Testament the centre is always found in God. So according to the New Testament we are brothers one to another only because we are all sons of God.

'For ye are all sons of God, through faith, in Christ Jesus.' So, unquestionably, as an examination of usage in the Greek New Testament shows, the words ought to read. Not, 'Ye are all sons of God through faith in Christ Jesus;' but 'Ye are all sons of God, through faith, in Christ Jesus.' We are sons of God not in our own right, but only because we are in Christ. Christ is the Son of God; if we are united to Him, if He is our great representative, we are sons of God in Him.

And we become sons of God, in this high Christian sense, not through our natural birth into the world, but through faith. Sonship towards God, like brotherhood between man and man, is not in the New Testament taken as a matter of course, but is put as something to be obtained. That is where the poignancy of apostolic teaching was to be found. We are too much inclined to assume nowadays that men are already sons of God; we are too much inclined to assume that all is well with their souls. The consequence is that they are not apt to be much interested in what we have to say. But the apostles were convinced of the desperate need of the world, of the dreadful separation between humanity and the righteous God. The gospel of Christ was the divinely appointed means by which men were to be brought in from the cold world of sin into the warmth and joy of God's house. When men listened to the message of Christ's grace and received in faith the gift which it announced to them, then and then only did they become sons of God. So it is also today, my friends. The gospel has not lost its power, but, alas, we are too well satisfied with the world and with sin. God grant that our satisfaction may be broken down, if we are not now in Christ; God grant that we may accept Christ's gift in faith and so may be no longer aliens and strangers but 'sons of God, through faith, in Christ Jesus.'

'For as many of you as were baptised into Christ did put on Christ.' Here the entrance into Christ and so into sonship towards God, which has just been said to be accomplished through faith, is declared to be enacted by baptism. Baptism seems here to be said to accomplish just what in the previous verse is said to be accomplished by faith. The apparent contradiction – if it be even apparent – leads to the true conception of what baptism is. Baptism, according to the New Testament, is primarily an outward sign of an inner change. It is more than a mere sign, since God has chosen to make this sign, together with the Lord's Supper, a special channel for the gracious power of His Spirit; but primarily it is a sign. To use a modern word (much overworked today, it is true) baptism 'visualises' faith. It 'signifies and seals our engrafting into Christ and our engagement to be the Lord's'.

'All you who have been baptised into Christ – have come by baptism into such a relation to Christ, that you can be said to be in Him – have put on Christ.' It is certainly a bold figure of speech. The Christian, says Paul, has clothed himself with Christ, has put on Christ as a garment. In the Old Testament, in several passages, one is said to clothe one's self with some virtue or quality – for example, in the One Hundred and Thirty-second Psalm: 'Let the priests be clothed with righteousness.' But here it is no one virtue with which Christians are said to be clothed, but with the whole glorious Person of Christ. It is a stupendous utterance. When one looks upon Christians, does one see just so many copies of Christ? To do so, alas, requires the eye of faith; too often Christians exhibit a life far short of the life of Him with whom they have been clothed. And in the Epistle to the Romans Paul has to urge his readers to do just what here is said to have been done already at baptism. There the readers are urged to 'put on' the Lord Jesus Christ; here they are said to have put on already the Lord Jesus Christ when they were baptised into Him. In Romans Paul is thinking of the realisation of this supreme relation to the Saviour in the hard battle of life in this world; here in Galatians he is thinking of the relationship as it exists in principle and in the sight of God. However it may be in the sight of men, when God looks upon Christians what He sees is not their own unworthiness and sinfulness but the glorious Person of Christ their representative and advocate and Saviour.

It is only on the basis of this bold intensity with which Paul conceives the intimate relation of believers to Christ that the apostle presents his ideal of solidarity among men: 'There can be neither Jew nor Greek, there can be neither bond nor free, there can be no male and female.' It is a great mistake to take that ideal as a matter of course; it is a great mistake to think that it can be realised simply by contemplation of life as we find it. At least that was not Paul's method, Paul's method was to seek the attainment of this ideal of solidarity of man with man not by the contemplation of human relations as they are but only by the stupendous work of the Spirit of God by which men were brought into a common union with Christ. In the world these distinctions of man from man still persist in all their divisions and destructive power, but in Christ they are done away.

'There can be neither Jew nor Greek, there can be neither bond nor free, there can be no male and female; for ye are all one person in Christ Jesus.' The Authorised Version says, 'Ye are all one in Christ Jesus.' But the true text is 'Ye are all one person.' The Person that is referred to is Christ. Christ is the only Person who really counts in the supreme relation to God. No matter what our position on earth may be, no matter what our social or racial relationships, we stand before God not by virtue of those relationships but because we are, if we be Christians, in Christ.

These words of Paul, if they stood alone, might be

taken in a mystical or pantheising sense, as though the Christian ideal were the loss of separate personality of the believer by merging in the life of Christ. But such an interpretation would be radically false. The apostle Paul was certainly not a mystic; he believed, it is true, in the direct communion of the soul with God; in that broad, popular sense of the word he was mystical. But that usage is misleading; and in the true sense of the word Paul was no mystic. He did not say that the Christians are identical with Christ; the relation of the believer with his Lord is, according to the Apostle, always the relation of one person to another Person. It is a relation not of mystical submerging but of personal love. Yet the relation, though not destructive of separate personality, is far more intimate than any relationship known between man and man upon the earth. The Christian is so closely united to Christ that he can be said to be 'in Christ'; he has put on Christ as a garment; and the whole body of Christians is one Person, so far as the supreme relation to God is concerned, because it is represented by the one Person Jesus Christ.

Such is the Christian ideal of brotherhood. It is not a brotherhood of man as man, but a brotherhood of the redeemed who are in Christ. Yet there is absolutely nothing narrow about this ideal. Brotherhood in this highest sense is restricted, indeed, to Christians, and if it is to mean anything there must be sharp separation between those who are Christians and those who are not. The household of faith is to be sharply distinguished from the world. But there is nothing narrow about that distinction; for the door of the household of faith is open wide, and all without exception are invited to come in. Christ died to open that door, and the chief business of God's children is to bring others through it into the brotherhood of the redeemed. The great trouble is not that we love those who are not Christians too much, but rather that we do not love them enough. If we really loved them, we should not be content with the relationship to them involved in the comparatively cold brotherhood of man, but we should long passionately, and by the preaching of the gospel we should make constant and earnest endeavour, to bring them in with us into the full intimacy of the household of God.

# 8: *The Claims of Love*

*'And being in Bethany in the house of Simon the leper, as he sat at meat, there came a woman having an alabaster box of ointment of spikenard very precious; and she brake the box, and poured it on his head. And there were some that had indignation within themselves, and said, Why was this waste of the ointment made? For it might have been sold for more than three hundred pence, and have been given to the poor. And they murmured against her. And Jesus said, Let her alone; why trouble ye her? she hath wrought a good work on me. For ye have the poor with you always, and whensoever ye will ye may do them good; but me ye have not always. She hath done what she could: she is come aforehand to anoint my body to the burying'* (Mark 14:3–8).

THIS incident delivers the Christian world from a crushing tyranny. There are many other forms of tyranny from which the Christian man is set free – the tyranny of guilt, the tyranny of the power of sin, the tyranny of fate. The tyranny from which this incident sets us free is different from these; yet it is a crushing bondage all the same. In these words to the woman at Bethany our Lord sets us free from the oppressive tyranny of the efficiency expert.

'Might it not have been sold for more than three hundred pence, and have been given to the poor?' Certainly it might. The price of the ointment amounted to the wage of a labourer for three hundred days; there were many poor people in Jerusalem who could well have used such a sum. Yet the precious box was emptied upon the head of Jesus as He sat at table in Simon's house, and the poor were allowed to remain in want. The slightest calculation might have led the woman to

67

act differently, but the point of the narrative is that she did not calculate at all. All that she saw was Jesus – the whole rest of the world was forgotten. There sat her dear Saviour and Lord, and her heart was full of reverence and love. What place was there for exact calculations as to the best use of funds, what place for aught save gratitude and honour for Him who was her only hope for time and for eternity? Little did she care for the cold criticism of the disciples; broken was the flask and the room filled with the lavish fragrance of the ointment. Calculation and efficiency were conquered by the might of love.

Do you think that we can learn anything in these days from that woman's act? Our Lord thought that we could. 'Wheresoever this gospel shall be preached', he said, 'throughout the whole world, this also that she hath done shall be spoken of for a memorial of her.' 'For a memorial of her' – yes, and also for an example to us. In these days of cold efficiency we need to learn the claims of love.

We need to learn the claims of love, first, in our own individual lives. Even service, no matter how efficient and how diligent it may be, cannot take the place of the deep affection of the heart. I am not forgetting those texts of Scripture where service is celebrated in the loftiest terms. 'Whosoever shall give to drink unto one of these little ones a cup of cold water only in the name of a disciple, verily I say unto you, he shall in no wise lose his reward.' 'Pure religion and undefiled before God and the Father is this, To visit the fatherless and widows in their affliction, and to keep himself unspotted from the world.' Certainly service is necessary to religion; but do you think that service is all that is necessary? I think not, my friends. I think that you will find if you read your Bible with sympathy and care that even service is comparatively useless unless it comes from the heart; true service is not a substitute for love, but the expression of love. 'And though I bestow all my goods to feed the poor, and though I give my body to be burned, and have not love, it profiteth me nothing.'

The love spoken of in the New Testament is not merely love of the brethren, but it is also love of Christ. We are sometimes inclined to ignore that fact; we are sometimes inclined to quote one text and not to quote also another text that God gave us as the supplement of the first. We are sometimes inclined to quote the words of Jesus in the twenty-fifth chapter of Matthew – 'Inasmuch as ye have done it unto one of the least of these my brethren, ye have done it unto me' – and to neglect the gracious words that have been read today. We are sometimes tempted to think that Christ is only a collective name for the totality of those who need our help; we lose sight of the central fact that He is a living Person. And in doing so we miss the centre and core of the Christian life.

The error can be avoided if we attend to the words of Jesus in the passage read today. If we are tempted to think that the service of the poor is all that there is in the service of Christ, if we are tempted to make of Christ a mere collective name and not an individual Person, then we should have recourse ever anew to this incident of the anointing at Bethany.

Here, in one of the most unforgettable, characteristic words that Jesus ever uttered, our Lord actually contrasts the service of the poor with the service of Him. 'Ye have the poor with you always,' he said, 'and whensoever ye will ye may do them good; but me ye have not always.' We have not Jesus always with us in the sense in which the woman had Him with her at Bethany; we cannot pour any precious ointment upon His head. But in a higher better sense we have Him with us still. And surely we must not neglect the privilege of communion with Him.

Certainly I am not advocating neglect of external service. Without that it is quite impossible that we should be true disciples of Jesus. It is a poor and untrue religion which leaves the hungry in distress. But we shall perform such service all the better if we take time also to commune with Jesus Himself. Do you think that the Christian life is concerned only with philanthropy; do you think that activity in social service is all that our Lord desires? Oh no, my friends. Those things are absolutely necessary to the Christian, but they are not all that is necessary. If we are true Christians, we shall not neglect those things; but we shall also take time to go into our closet and close the door; and there, with the world shut out, with even our service forgotten for the moment, we shall think no longer of what we do but of what our Saviour has done, and we shall pour out upon Him, with an abandon like that of the woman at Bethany, our gratitude and love and praise.

What did Jesus say about that woman? We have reviewed part of what He said. But the most important part is yet untouched. 'She hath done what she could,' said Jesus: 'she is come aforehand to anoint my body to the burying.' There is the centre of the incident, and the centre here as well as elsewhere is found at Calvary. The woman probably did not know about our Lord's approaching death, but Jesus knew; and, in a word of beauty unsurpassed, he placed that woman's act at the beginning of the long series of acts of love and gratitude in which Christians throughout the centuries have celebrated the cross. Jesus did not go to Jerusalem to bring about a revolution or a reformation; he went there to die for the sins of the world; and when the woman, forgetting all calculations, forgetting the cold criticism of those who stood by, poured out the precious ointment upon His head, He took it as the response of the human heart to His redeeming love. 'She is come aforehand to anoint my body to the burying.' 'Wheresoever this gospel shall be preached throughout the whole world, this also that she hath done shall be spoken of for a memorial of her.'

Let us take the example to our hearts; let us not be

so engrossed in our service that we forget our Saviour's love; let us not forget to pour out upon Him, in the secret place of prayer, the vials of our gratitude and praise. The woman anointed Him aforehand for the burial; we look back upon His completed work in which He loved us and gave Himself for us. Let us not through overmuch serving forget the better part; let us rather bring service forth from the contemplation of the cross.

> *O dearly, dearly has He loved*
> *And we must love Him too,*
> *And trust in His redeeming blood,*
> *And try His works to do.*

Calculation in its place is good; but away with calculation if it hinders love!

But we need to recognise the claims of love not only in our own individual lives, but also in the collective work of the Church. The Church to which I belong – and it is the same with other similar bodies – has come to be a powerful organisation. It carries on the most varied work in all parts of the world; it conducts a great publication agency, and a great chain of bookshops with a huge volume of business; it maintains many scores of hospitals and colleges and institutes of all sorts at home and abroad; one can scarcely embrace in a single view all of its vast and varied service. Certainly such an enterprise cannot be conducted without business organisation; and I certainly am not advocating any diminution of efficiency. I am not even advocating for the moment any particular changes in the form of the organisation. I do indeed believe that the organisation of the church is becoming dangerously over-centralised. The church, it seems to me, is falling into somewhat the same error as the State – the State with its vast bureaus at Washington which, I am constrained to believe, with their discouragement of local initiative, their materialistic paternalism, are sucking the life-blood of the people. But such questions cannot be discussed now; they are matters of personal opinion in the preacher. What *is* clear, at any rate, is that any organisation, however good, is a menace if it becomes an end in itself and if it ceases to subserve the end which justifies its existence. And that danger of forgetting the end in the means, I am convinced, is menacing very seriously the life of the church of today. Yet there are hopeful signs of a change.

Some years ago the church seemed to me to be interested in nothing in the world except money. Great spiritual questions were shunted aside; the councils of the churches discussed methods of preaching, but seemed to be totally unwilling to attend at all to the question what it is that is to be preached.

But since that time there has come, in some quarters at least, a striking change. The churches a few years ago discussed money and questions of organisation but now they are discussing, to some extent at least, the basis of the Christian faith. There are many who deprecate the change; there are many who deprecate the discussion; there are many who say, 'Let the constructive work of the church go on irrespective of doctrinal differences.' But of course that begs the whole question. The question is just exactly what the constructive work of the church is. According to the Bible, the constructive work of the church is found in the propagation of a message – call it a doctrine if you will – a message in which Jesus is offered as the Saviour of men. If the church is propagating that message, well and good; then we are interested in having it as well organised as it possibly can be; but if it is not propagating that message, then we care little whether it is well organised or not. One cannot possibly avoid the basic question what it is that the church is in the world to do. A church that does not stop to examine itself, that does not stop ever and again to examine the basis of its life, is in danger of death.

A great movement, it seems to me, is now going

forward in many churches – a reaction against machinery, a recourse to what is central, and particularly a return to the cross of Christ. Some men stand coldly aside; they are deterred by obvious imperfections in the leaders of the movement; they refuse to be shaken out of the even tenor of the way into which they are fallen. It sounds so strange sometimes – this word of the cross! There is much opposition to the movement. But pray God that it may make its way! It is very pleasant to discuss merely ways and means and business methods and keep dangerous doctrinal questions in the background. Great, truly, in our day is the offence of the cross. But there are those whose hearts have been touched. The dear Lord died for them upon the cross, and even amid all the machinery of ecclesiastical business they cannot forget what He has done. The bystanders murmur at their unconventional acts; the bystanders talk of efficiency and of 'constructive work.' But what says the Lord Himself? There, my friends, is the real question. He commended the woman at Bethany, despite her inefficiency and her waste, when she proclaimed His death afore. Perhaps He may commend you, if, in our day, despite sins and imperfections, yet out of a heart overflowing with love, you seek amid committees and machinery and boards to put back into its rightful place the wondrous cross of Jesus our dear Saviour and Lord.

# 9: *The Living Saviour*

*'And Jesus went about all Galilee, teaching in their syn-
agogues, and preaching the gospel of the kingdom, and healing
all manner of sickness and all manner of disease among the
people'* (Matt. 4:23).
*'Lo, I am with you alway, even unto the end of the world'*
(Matt. 28:20b).

IN the synagogue at Capernaum there was a new
teaching. He speaks, they said, as one having authority,
and not as the scribes. There, we are sometimes led to
believe, is the origin of the religion we profess. 'Give us
that authority, and we can banish speculation. Jesus
taught a way of life; let us walk in it and leave
speculation to the philosophers. Jesus seemed to have
no fear of the inscrutable power that rules the world;
let us simply walk in His footsteps and be equally
fearless.' A simple programme, and one that seems full
of promise! But there is one trouble with it – it does not
work. The imitation of Jesus has never yet been carried
out. As a mere ideal, Jesus is a failure.

A failure, first of all, because of the very nature of an
ideal. An ideal must of necessity be insufficient, if it be
made the sole basis of life. Even this matchless ideal is
insufficient, it often leaves us without guidance. True,
Jesus enunciated some very far-reaching principles;
put the Sermon on the Mount into practice, do as well
as hear, and society will indeed be founded on the rock.
But the process of application is often very difficult.
Modern life is complex. Whole departments of life seem
to be neglected in the words of Jesus. What about man's
relation to the State? 'Render unto Caesar the things

that are Caesar's'? A pregnant saying, but surpassingly difficult to apply! Is the modern State to be treated like Caesar? What about art? Jesus did not despise it, for He spoke the parables. But what place should it have in human life, and how is it to be related to morality and to religion? And, to come nearer home, what of the nameless, concrete problems of individual life? Study the ethical principles of Jesus all you please, and still you will often be in hopeless perplexity. As a mere ideal – let us say it bluntly – as a mere ideal, Jesus is simply insufficient. And as an ideal, He is also powerless. The ideal is one that can never be attained – because of human weakness. A strange fact, but an undoubted one; a fact of experience! When we wish to do good, evil is present with us. Sin is no mere collective name for a chance succession of wrong actions, but a mighty unitary, spiritual power of evil. In the presence of it, we are helpless; it drags us back into the mire; it obscures the blessed vision with a black pall of despair. To talk about an ideal to a man under the thraldom of sin is a cruel mockery.

As a mere ideal, Jesus is a failure. But He never was content to be a mere ideal. And none of His contemporaries thought of Him as such. True, in that synagogue at Capernaum, they did think of Him as an ideal, as an example; they marvelled at His teaching. He spoke as one having authority and not as the scribes. But that was not the only cause of wonder. 'He commands even the unclean spirits and they obey him'! From the first, Jesus appeared not merely as a teacher, but also as a healer; He brought not merely guidance, but active help; He had not merely authority, but also power.

Jesus the great physician! The great healer of every sickness and every infirmity! The blind receive their sight, and the lame walk, the lepers are cleansed, and the deaf hear. And this cure of bodily ills was but a sign and proof and seal of the healing of the soul. He who said, 'I will, be thou clean,' said also, 'Thy sins are forgiven thee.' Jesus the healer of souls! God knows, we need Him still. When past sins rise up to mock our best endeavours, when our strength is sapped by the power of evil, when our lives seem to be a hopeless tangle, unlike anything that was ever seen before, escape shut off on every side, regret and remorse staring us in the face whichever turn we take, a strange miserable hopeless puzzle, beyond our own comprehension and far beyond our own power to help – we need a healer. We need one who knows us better than we know ourselves, one who can untangle the snarl of our lives, who can apply a healing touch to the dreadful wounds of the soul, and set us forward in some new, strong, healthy life.

A healer – where shall we find him? A few men and women found such an one long ago in Palestine. A paralytic borne of four – 'Child, thy sins are forgiven thee.' A publican sitting at the receipt of custom – 'They that are whole need not a physician, but they that are sick.' A demoniac among the tombs, whom they found sitting clothed and in his right mind. A sick woman, who touched His garment – 'Daughter, thy faith hath saved thee; go in peace.' These, somehow we are sure of it, received peace. They found a healer.

But we! Where shall we find him? This Jesus of Nazareth died these nineteen hundred years ago. And there is none to take His place. Compare with Him the men of the present day, even the best of them, and we are in despair. For the people of ancient Galilee, life's problem was easy; they needed only to push in through the crowd or be lowered through some Capernaum roof, and the long search was over. But we are separated by nineteen centuries from this One who alone could give us aid. How can we bridge the gulf of time that separates us from Jesus?

Now some people regard it as a very simple matter. 'Jesus is not dead,' we are told, 'He lives on through His recorded words and deeds. We do not need even to believe it all; even a part is sufficient; the wonderful personality of Jesus shines out clear from the Gospel story. Jesus may still be known. Let us simply – without speculation, without theology – abandon ourselves to His spell, and He will heal us.'

There is a certain plausibility about that. It may readily be admitted that Jesus lives on in the Gospel record. In that narrative, we see not merely a lifeless picture; we receive the impression of a living person. We can still share the astonishment of those who listened to the new teaching in the synagogue at Capernaum. We can sympathise with the faith and devotion of the little band of disciples who would not leave Him when others were offended at the hard saying. We feel a sympathetic thrill of joy at the blessed relief which was given to men who were sick in body and mind. We can appreciate the wonderful love and compassion of Him who was sent to seek and to save that which was lost. A wonderful story indeed, not dead, but pulsating with life at every turn!

The Jesus of the Gospels is a real, a living person. But that is not the only question. We are going forward far too fast. Another question remains. Jesus lives in the Gospels. But we of the twentieth century, how may we come into vital relation to Him? There is the real question. He died nineteen hundred years ago. The life which He now lives in the Gospels is simply the old life over and over again. And in that life we have no place; in that life we are spectators, not actors. The life which Jesus lives in the Gospels is, after all, for us but the spurious life of the stage. We sit silent in the playhouse, and watch the absorbing gospel drama of forgiveness and healing and love and courage and high endeavour. In rapt attention we follow the fortunes of those who came to Jesus labouring and heavy-laden and found rest. For a time our own troubles are forgotten. But suddenly the curtain falls, and out we go again into the cold humdrum of our own lives. Gone are the warmth and gladness of an ideal world. 'In their stead a sense of real things comes doubly strong.' We are no longer living over again the lives of Peter and James and John. Alas, we are living our own lives once more, with our own problems and our own misery and our own sin. And still we are seeking our own Saviour.

Let us not deceive ourselves. A Jewish teacher of the first century can never satisfy the longing of our souls. Clothe him with all the art of modern research, throw upon him the warm deceptive calcium-light of modern sentimentality, and despite it all common sense will come to her rights again, and for our brief hour of self-deception will wreak upon us the revenge of hopeless disillusionment.

But, says the modern theologian, are we not, in rejecting theology, in being satisfied with the historical Jesus, merely restoring the simplicity of the primitive gospel? No, we answer, you are not, but you are not so very far wrong. You are really returning to a very primitive stage in the life of the church. But that stage is not the 'Galilean springtime,' for in Galilee men had a living Saviour. There was one time, and one time only, when the disciples lived, like you, merely on the memory of Jesus. When was it? It was a gloomy, desperate time – it was the three sad days after the crucifixion. Then and then only did Jesus' disciples regard Him merely as a blessed memory: 'We hoped that it was he which should redeem Israel.' Shall we remain forever in the gloom of those sad days, or shall we pass out from them to the warmth and joy of Pentecost?

Let us not deceive ourselves. We shall remain forever in the gloom unless we take one decisive step. We may have joy for sadness and power for weakness. But not by easy halfway measures, not by compromise with the wisdom of the world, but only by a divine radicalism, only by one stupendous act of faith. What was it that within a few days transformed that humble band of mourners, after the crucifixion of Jesus, into the spiritual conquerors of the world? History is relentlessly plain. Whatever it was, it was not the memory of Jesus' life. That was a source of sadness, not of joy. It was one thing, and one thing only: It was the message, 'He is risen.'

That message is despised today. Science, flushed with conquest, grown over-bold, would relegate it to the limbo of discarded fancies. Even the church would do without it. Jesus is dead, we are told, but we must treat Him as though He were alive. An heroic effort! To it have been devoted the resources of modern scholarship. But a failure! Despite it all, the power of the church, under such treatment, is slowly but steadily declining. And no wonder! False sentimentality is no conqueror. If Jesus is dead, He must be treated as dead. This question must be faced: Give Jesus up, or believe that He rose from the dead. It is not easy to believe; the resurrection can no longer be accepted as a matter of course. Against it are arrayed mighty resources of modern culture. Traditional, second-hand faith is rapidly being swept away. Faith, in this age, must be of sterner stuff. If it is retained by ignoring facts, it may be useful to the individual, but it will never conquer the world. But there is another kind of faith. Faith that does not ignore the findings of modern science, but supplements them. Faith that sweeps away the superficial technicalities of research, and faces the persistent, underlying facts – the fact of sin; the sinless, unearthly character of Jesus; His mysterious self-consciousness; the testimony of the disciples; the empty tomb; the very origin of the Christian church; the glories of Christian experience. Attend to these facts, and you will believe in the resurrection. It is not easy to believe. And we need not regret it. An easy faith would never conquer the world. The resurrection can at least no longer be accepted as a commonplace thing. If a fact, it brings us today as never before into naked connection with the ultimate mystery. Faith is no longer easy to attain. But once attained it is doubly worth a battle.

If we believe that Jesus rose from the dead, we can have hope. A Saviour lives! But the religious problem of our lives has not yet been solved. An historical conviction of the resurrection of Jesus is not the end of faith, but only the beginning. If faith stops there, I fear it will never stand the fires of criticism. Jesus lives. But what good is it to us? We are like the inhabitants of far-off Syria. The fame of Him has gone abroad; there was a prophet in Galilee who could heal every ill of body and mind, and we are told that He still lives. But, alas, we are not with Him, and the way is far. Jesus lives. But that is not enough. He lives, and we are told that He has healing for us. But before we can be healed we must find Him.

How shall we find Him? There is the problem. You and I who sit in this house today, how shall we find that Jesus who lived and died and is declared to live again. Surely it is not so very plain. We cannot find Him in crowded houses or by the lake-shore or in desert places; we cannot be lowered through the roof into any room where He sits amid scribes and Pharisees. If we employ only our own methods of search, we shall find ourselves on a never-ending, fruitless pilgrimage. Surely we need instruction.

And in the New Testament we find instruction, full and free. What, in a word, does the New Testament say about the way of approach to Jesus?

In the New Testament, a strange fact stares us in the face – the New Testament seems far more concerned with the death of Jesus than with the details of His life. Learned men have tried in vain to explain that curious fact; in long and weary treatises they have sought the explanation. But the explanation is really so simple that a child can understand it. The New Testament emphasises the death of Jesus because that is what Jesus did for us. In the account of the details of Jesus' life, we are told what He did for others. That account is indeed absolutely necessary, so necessary that it is always presupposed; without it we should never have become interested in Jesus at all. But it is to us a means to an end, not an end in itself. We read in the Gospels what Jesus did for others. For one He placed His fingers in the ears, and said, 'Be opened;' to another, 'Arise, take up thy bed and walk;' to another, 'Lazarus, come forth;' to another, 'Thy sins are forgiven thee.' These things are what Jesus did for others. But what will He do, or what has He done, for us? The answer of the New Testament is plain. For us, He does not say, 'Arise and walk.' For us, He did a greater thing; for us, He died. That mysterious thing that was wrought on Calvary, that was His work for us. The cross of Christ is a mystery. In the presence of it theology walks, after all, with but trembling, halting footsteps. Learning alone will never unlock its meaning. But to the penitent sinner, though mysterious, though full of baffling riddles, it is plain *enough*. On the cross Jesus dealt with our sin. Our dreadful guilt, the condemnation of God's law – it is wiped out by an act of grace. It seemed absolutely inseparable from us; it was a burden no earthly friend could bear. But Christ is master of the innermost secrets of the moral world; with Him all things are possible; He has accomplished the impossible; He has borne our sin!

But through whom does He apply His healing touch? Through no one, save His own Spirit. Christ needs no intermediary, for He is here Himself. By His resurrection and ascension He has entered, with silent footsteps, into the lives of every one of us. He is no longer, as in Galilee, bound by limitations of time and space. 'The Lord is the Spirit.' We need not stir from this house; we need not even bow our heads in prayer. If we are really seekers for Him, then this moment our search is over.

And as we go from the place of worship, our lives will be different. True, we shall have only the same guides as before – the same Bible, and in the life of Jesus the same ideal. But the ideal was insufficient before, and powerless. Now it is all-sufficient, and more powerful than all the forces of the adversary. We had the ideal before, but were unable to interpret it; now we have a living Teacher. We had the ideal before, but could not put it into practice; now we have a Helper. The modern theologians are right in looking to Jesus of Nazareth for the inspiration of life and the foundation of society. But not to a Jesus who is dead. Look to the Sermon on the Mount for the supreme guide of your life; it is sufficient for all needs; it is sufficient for the most complex of modern problems. But not as a mere code of law. Hear the Sermon on the Mount, and your life will be founded on the rock. But hear it, not from a dead teacher, but ever anew from the crucified and risen Lord.

Our lives have been different since Jesus entered in. But one dreadful doubt assails us. Jesus has carried us far. But has He carried us all the way? He has helped. But we had other helpers too. We had other helpers, but they left us dissatisfied. Jesus has done more than they. But has He done all? Jesus of Nazareth seems to belong after all to this earth. And what of the dread thought of infinity?

Reflections on the nothingness of human life are often rather dull; they clothe themselves readily in cant. But if a thing is true, it cannot become false by being hackneyed. Man is imprisoned on one of the smaller of the planets; he is enveloped by infinity on all sides; and he lives but for a day in a pitiless procession. The things in which he is interested, the whole of his world, form but an imperceptible oasis in the desert of immensity. Strange that he can be absorbed in things which from the vantage-ground of infinity must seem smaller than the smallest playthings.

It cannot be denied. Man is a poor finite creature; he is a denizen of the earth. From one point of view, he is very much like the beasts that perish. Like them, he lives in a world of phenomena; he is subject to a succession of experiences, and he does not understand any one of them. Science can observe; it cannot explain. When it tries to explain, it becomes laughable. Man is certainly finite. But that is not the whole truth. He is not only finite, for he knows that he is finite, and that knowledge brings him into connection with infinity. He lives in a finite world. But he knows at least that it is not the totality of things. He lives in a procession of phenomena. But to save his life he cannot help searching for a first cause. In the midst of his trivial life, there rises in his mind one strange and overpowering thought – the thought of God. It may come by reflection, by subtle argument – from effect to cause, from the design to the designer. Or it may come by 'a sunset touch.' Back of the red, mysterious, terrible, silent depths, beyond the silent meeting-place of sea and sky, there is an inscrutable power. In the presence of it we are helpless as a stick or stone. As helpless, but more unhappy – unhappy because of fear. With what assurance can we meet the infinite power? Its works in nature are horrible in the infliction of suffering. And what if physical suffering should not be all, what of the sense of guilt? What if the condemnation of conscience should be but the foretaste of judgment? What if contact with the infinite should be contact with a dreadful infinity of holiness? What if the inscrutable cause of all things should turn out to be, after all, a righteous God.

This great beyond of mystery – can Jesus help us there? Make Jesus as great as you will, and still He seems insufficient. Extend the domains of His power far beyond our ken, and still there is a shelving brink with the infinite beyond. And still we are subject to fear. The mysterious power that explains the world, still it will sweep in one day and engulf us and our Saviour alike. We are of all men most miserable.

We had trusted in Jesus. He carried us a little on our

way, and then left us helpless as before, on the brink of eternity. There is for us no hope; we stand defenceless at length in the presence of unfathomed mystery, unless – a wild, fantastic thought – unless this Jesus, our Saviour in whom we had trusted, were Himself in mysterious union with the eternal God. The puzzling sentence in Philippians, 'Who, being in the form of God, thought it not robbery to be equal with God'; the strange cosmology of Colossians, 'who is the image of the invisible God, the firstborn of every creature: for by him were all things created, that are in heaven, and that are in earth, visible and invisible, whether they be thrones, or dominions, or principalities, or powers: all things were created by him, and for him: and he is before all things, and by him all things consist'; the majestic prologue of the Fourth Gospel, 'In the beginning was the Word, and the Word was with God, and the Word was God'; the mysterious consciousness of Jesus, 'All things are delivered unto me of my Father: and no man knoweth the Son, but the Father; neither knoweth any man the Father, save the Son, and he to whomsoever the Son will reveal him'; 'I and my Father are one.' These things have been despised as idle speculation, as 'theology'.

In reality, they are the very breath of our lives. They are the battleground of theologians; the church hurled anathemas at those who held that Christ, though great, was less than God. And rightly! That difference was no trifle. There is no such thing as 'almost God.' The thought is blasphemy. The next thing less than the infinite is infinitely less. If Christ be the greatest of finite creatures, then still our souls are restless, still we are seekers after God. But now is Christ, our Saviour, our Champion, the same who says, 'Thy sins are forgiven thee,' revealed as very God. And we believe! It is the supreme venture of faith; faith can go no higher.

Such a faith is a constant mystery to us who possess

it; it is ridiculed by those who have it not. But, if possessed, it overcomes the world. In Christ, all things are ours. There is now no awful beyond of mystery and fear. We cannot explain the world. But we rejoice now that we cannot explain it. To us it is all unknown. But it contains no mysteries for our Saviour. He is on the throne. He is at the centre. He is ground and explanation of all things. He pervades the remotest bounds. In Him all things consist. The world is full of dread, mysterious powers. They touch us already in a thousand woes. But from all of them we are safe. 'Who shall separate us from the love of Christ? shall tribulation, or distress, or persecution, or famine, or nakedness, or peril, or sword? As it is written, For thy sake we are killed all the day long; we are accounted as sheep for the slaughter. Nay, in all these things we are more than conquerors through him that loved us. For I am persuaded, that neither death, nor life, nor angels, nor principalities, nor powers, nor things present, nor things to come, nor height, nor depth, nor any other creature, shall be able to separate us from the love of God, which is in Christ Jesus our Lord.'

# 10: *Justified by Faith*

*'Therefore being justified by faith, we have peace with God through our Lord Jesus Christ'* (Rom. 5:1).

THE doctrine of justification by faith alone is the very foundation of our Protestant life. It had been obscured in the Middle Ages by the Church of Rome. In practice even more than in theory salvation had been made to depend upon obedience to an elaborate set of rules prescribed by the Church. The result was an intolerable bondage. But in God's good time the deliverer was raised up. A monk by the name of Martin Luther began to read the Epistle to the Galatians with his own eyes, and evangelical liberty was born. It is a great mistake to suppose that Luther was merely an emancipator; it is a great mistake to regard him as a spiritual brother of those who have sought liberty for its own sake, or of those who have founded liberty merely upon the inherent rights of man. On the contrary Luther founded liberty not upon a right which man possessed as man, but upon a right which was conferred upon him by God. Luther combated the doctrine of the Church of Rome not by advocating indifference to doctrine but by championing another and an older doctrine; he appealed against the tradition of Rome not to the desires of men's hearts but to what God had revealed; he advocated as over against the authority of the Church, not the absence of all authority but the authority of the Bible as the Word of God. In particular, he set up against the doctrine of submission to the Church the great Protestant doctrine of justification by faith.

There were others at the time of Luther who assumed

a very different attitude; there were those who at bottom had an antipathy to the doctrine of Rome not because they were devoted to a contrary doctrine but because they were at heart opposed to all doctrine; there were those who would have been glad to fight false doctrine not by true doctrine but by agnosticism. Such perhaps was in spirit at least the position of the great Erasmus, the foremost scholar of the age. I say 'perhaps', because I confess that in judging Erasmus I am just now somewhat under the spell of Froude. Froude was himself a sceptic; it is possible therefore that he was inclined to make his hero too much like himself. But on the whole Froude's *Life and Letters of Erasmus* is rather a convincing book. It pictures the great scholar of the Reformation period as being at heart, though of course not consciously or explicitly, a precursor of the non-doctrinal Christianity so popular at the present day. And whatever may finally be thought of the picture, it has a certain amount of *prima facie* evidence in its favour. Erasmus will always be known to history as the man who would not take sides. There was in his day a great spiritual conflict, the greatest that the world had known for fifteen centuries. Erasmus certainly contributed to the outbreak of it, but he would not accept the final consequences of his own work; he would not fight in the van of the battle, and finally he retired to an inglorious life in the rear.

Erasmus has been blamed for cowardice, and the adjective 'Erasmian' derived from his name has a somewhat evil sound. But perhaps the charge does him injustice, or rather the charge of cowardice blames Erasmus for a fault different from the one which was actually his. Certainly the indecision of that great scholar was an inglorious thing; though he did not like the abuses of the Roman system yet he would not side with Luther in his heroic fight. But his indecision was perhaps not due to cowardice; it was rather due to an absence of conviction. His fault was not that being convinced of the truth of the Reformation doctrine he concealed his conviction from fear of men; but rather that he was not convinced at all. Thus he went with the Reformation in its negative work; he joined with it in attacking the abuses of the Church of Rome. But he differed from the Reformation in having nothing positive to put in the place of that which was destroyed.

The choice between Luther and Erasmus had to be made in the sixteenth century and the same choice has to be made today. There are those who believe that the search for objective truth in religion must be abandoned, that doctrine is merely the necessarily changing form in which religious experience is expressed, and that a humanistic eclecticism is the highest ideal. But there are also those who with Luther combat error not in the interests of negation but in the interests of truth; there are those who like Luther have a message and are willing to stand for it against the world.

What then was the message of Luther which set the world aflame? It was not something that Luther originated but something that he discovered; the Reformation of the sixteenth century was a rediscovery of Paul, and through Paul a rediscovery of Jesus.

At the centre of the message was the doctrine of justification by faith. Some men would be horrified by this use of a theological term; they seem to have a notion that modern Christians must be addressed always in words of one syllable, and that in religion the scientific precision of language which is found so useful in other spheres must be abandoned. I am by no means ready to agree. It is perfectly true that the Bible and the people ought to be brought together. But what is not always observed is that there are two ways of achieving that end. One way is to bring the Bible down to the level of the people; the other way is to let the people be lifted up to the level of the Bible. For my part, I prefer the latter way. I am by no means ready to relinquish the advantages of a precise terminology in summarising Bible truth. In religion as well as in other spheres a precise terminology is mentally economical in the end; it repays amply the slight effort required for the mastery of it. It should be used even in many cases where it is not found in the Bible itself, but only summarises what the Bible teaches. But in the case of 'justification by faith,' the terminology most emphatically is found in the Bible; and when Professor Goodspeed in his translation of the New Testament renders the word which means 'justify' by 'make upright', he is misrepresenting at its very centre the book which he is purporting to translate. One may well be appalled by the religious retrogression which is involved in that translation; for by it the entire achievement of the Reformation is abandoned, and there is a return to the merit-religion of the Middle Ages. But what is almost equally appalling, perhaps, is the abandonment of the historical method which is involved in this modernising of the Apostle Paul. It may be that the modern translator is not much interested in justification by faith; but every true historian must surely admit that Paul was interested in it, and a translator, if he be true to his sacred trust, must place the emphasis, not where he could wish it placed, but where it actually was placed by the writer whose thought he is trying to reproduce. From every point of view, therefore, the terminology of Paul should be retained. I am not one bit ashamed to speak of 'the doctrine of justification by faith.'

But let us not suppose for a moment that that doctrine is an abstruse or intricate thing. On the contrary it is a very simple thing and it is instinct with life.

It is an answer to the greatest personal question ever asked by a human soul – the question, 'How shall I be right with God?', 'How do I stand in God's sight, with what favour does He look upon me?' There are those, I admit, who never raise that question; there are those who are concerned with the question of their standing before men but never with the question of their standing before God; there are those who are interested in what 'people say' but not in the question what God says. Such men, however, are not those who move the world: they are apt to go with the current; they are apt to do as others do; they are not the heroes who change the destinies of the race. The beginning of true nobility comes when a man ceases to be interested in the judgment of men and becomes interested in the judgment of God.

But if we can gain that much insight: if we have become interested in the judgment of God, how shall we stand in that judgment? How shall we become right with God? The most obvious answer is, By obeying God's law, by being what God wants us to be. There is absolutely nothing wrong in theory about the answer; the only trouble is that for us it does not work. If we had obeyed the law of God, if we were what God wants us to be, all would no doubt be well; we could approach the judgment seat of God and trust simply in God's just recognition of the facts. But, alas, we have not obeyed God's law, but transgressed it in thought, word and deed; and far from being what God wants us to be we are stained and soiled with sin. The stain is not merely on the surface; it is not a thing which can be wiped off by a damp cloth; but it permeates the recesses of our souls. And the clearer be our understanding of God's law, the deeper becomes our despair. Some men seek a refuge from condemnation by a low view of the law of God; they limit the law to external commands and by obeying those commands they hope to buy God's favour. But the moment a man gains a view of the law as it is – especially as it is revealed in the words and example of Jesus – at that moment he knows that he is undone. If our being right with God depends upon anything that is in us, we are without hope.

But another way into God's presence has been opened, and the opening of that way is set forth in the gospel. We deserve eternal death; we deserve exclusion from

God's righteous presence; but the Lord Jesus took upon Himself all the guilt of our sins and died instead of us on the cross. Henceforth the law's demands have been satisfied for us by Christ, its terror for us is gone, and clothed no longer in our righteousness but in the righteousness of Christ we stand without fear as Christ would stand without fear before the judgment seat of God. Men say that that is an intricate theory of the atonement; but surely the adjective is misplaced. It is mysterious, but it is not intricate; it is wonderful, but it is so simple that a child can understand.

No doubt the application of this redeeming work of Christ to the individual soul is mysterious enough. It is far beyond the wisdom and power of man. It is not a thing that can be effected by human reasoning or human effort; the beginning of the Christian life is not an achievement but an experience. Those who have passed through that experience are new creatures; they wonder at their former blindness; they wonder how there ever could have been a time when, with the scoffing world, they did not understand. The beginning of the Christian life is not an act of man but a wonderful act of the Spirit of God.

But it is accompanied by a conscious act of man; it is accompanied by the act of faith. Faith is not a meritorious work; the New Testament never says that a man is saved on account of his faith, but always that he is saved through his faith. Faith is the means which the Holy Spirit uses to apply to the individual soul the benefits of Christ's death.

And faith is a very simple thing; it simply means the receiving of a gift; it simply means that abandoning the vain effort of earning our way into God's presence we accept the gift of salvation which Christ offers so full and free. Such is the doctrine – let us not be afraid of the word – such is the doctrine of justification by faith.

That has been a liberating doctrine; to it is due most

of the freedom that we possess today, and if it is abandoned freedom will soon depart. If we are interested in what God thinks of us, we shall not be deterred by what men think; the very desire for justification before God makes us independent of the judgments of men. And if the very desire for justification is liberating, how much more the attainment of it! The man who has been justified by God, the man who has accepted as a free gift this condition of rightness with God, is not a man who hopes that possibly, with due effort, if he does not fail, he may win through to become a child of God. But he is a man who has already become a child of God. If our being children of God depended in the slightest measure upon ourselves, we could never be sure that we had attained the high estate. But it does not depend upon ourselves; it depends only upon God. It is not a reward that we have earned but a gift that we received.

A hard battle indeed lies before us. This faith of ours, if we be true Christians, is a faith that works; and it is a faith that fights – against sin. But we begin the battle not with God as our reward, but with God as our ally. There is the high liberty of the Christian man. Let us not throw our liberty away; let us not descend into the bondage of dependence upon ourselves, let us not descend into the hard bondage of agnostic Modernism. But having received the gospel – this great Magna Charta of Christian liberty – let us stand fast in the liberty wherewith Christ has set us free.

# 11: *The Gospel and Modern Substitutes*

*'I am not ashamed of the gospel'* (Rom. 1:16).

PAUL was not ashamed of the gospel of Christ, but a good many people nowadays are ashamed of it. At least the Epistle to the Romans, in which more fully than in any other book of the Bible, that gospel is set forth, is not altogether a popular book. And the reason why it is unpopular is perfectly plain – it is unpopular because it is so disturbingly definite. Paul had one thing, and one thing only, to say about the way of salvation. His programme of religious work was very simple and very uncompromising. He had no sympathy with what J. S. Phillimore has aptly called, 'The courtly polygamies of the soul.' For him there was one Lord and Master and one only – namely, Jesus Christ. Paul had no sympathy with the notion that religion is something to be kept in the background of life and that there is such a thing as being 'too religious.' The Religious Work Programme of the Y.M.C.A. may be made too prominent, say some, so as to discourage men who are interested in the welfare of mankind and yet are not willing to commit their all to Jesus Christ, who died for all men. But Paul would not have recognised the Y.M.C.A. as Christian, if it keeps its 'Religious Work Programme,' as we say in modern phraseology, in the background and does not make it the whole of what it is trying to do. Salvation according to Paul was to be found only in the atoning death of the Lord Jesus Christ, applied by the Holy Spirit of God and received through faith.

But if a modern leader of the church had found himself in the place where the Apostle Paul found himself when that letter was written, it would have been a different letter that would have been produced, because at the present time men are inclined to be very apologetic and very concessive about their Christianity. They are perfectly willing to admit that this may be one way in which other people are helped, but if other people are helped in some different way, we are as far as possible, men say today, from trying to make our way theirs. If you had found the leader of a modern church in the place in which Paul found himself when this letter was written, a very different letter would have been produced. Paul was preparing for his coming to the city of Rome, and it was the time to put his best foot forward – a time to win adherents to his cause by a concessive attitude. The modern leader would have said: 'Paul, to all those at Rome who are leading the Christ life, whatever may be the name by which they are called and whatever may be their creed, Greeting: I rejoice when I hear of your noble Christian service, and I long to see you, that you and I may talk over together methods of Christian work. Unfortunately, circumstances have prevented, but I hope at least to be able to see you. For I am not ashamed of the gospel that I preach, because I believe that with careful handling, if emphasis be laid upon the points where it is agreed with other faiths and if controversial matters be kept carefully in the background, I believe that the gospel that I preach may safely be proclaimed without creating too much trouble, even in the city of Rome.'

This is the beginning of the modern Epistle to the Romans. It is true, our modern Paul would have had a great deal of explaining to do. And the rest of the letter would have had to run something like this: 'It is true,' our modern Paul would have had to say, 'in Galatia unfortunate anathemas were pronounced against those who were proclaiming a different gospel. Now, when we come to Rome, we want to make it perfectly plain that if the Jews can obtain any help from conforming to the Mosaic law as one of the means of salvation, we shall not interfere with them. At Ephesus, the unfortunate impression was produced that our gospel was interfering with the worship of Diana of the Ephesians. Now we want to make it plain when we come to Rome that if one man can obtain contact with the divine through plastic representations commonly called idols, we are as far as possible from wanting to interfere with his faith. At Thessalonica, something unfortunate was said about turning from idols to serve the living God. Now when we come to Rome we want to make it plain that we are not asking any man to turn from anything. We are not giving a man a new creed, but we are merely trying to help him make effective in his life whatever creed he may chance to have.'

That is the modern Epistle to the Romans. Sermons are being preached from it in thousands of pulpits today.

But I call your attention to this fact, that if the Epistle to the Romans be re-written in this way, – and as a matter of fact it is not only the Epistle to the Romans that has to be rewritten, but also the teachings of Jesus – if it is to be rewritten in this way, the actual Epistle disappears. In fact the whole Bible disappears. The beginning of the Epistle to the Romans is particularly unfortunate from this modern concessive point of view, because Paul does not begin with mere general principles of religion – after the manner of those modern men who hold that back of Christianity and all positive faith you have some certain general principles of religion that you can get at and that men can agree on, so that people will say: 'We can agree upon certain permanent general principles of religion.' Paul thought general principles of religion were the most gloomy and hopeless things in the world. He thought that if we were dependent upon things which always were true, general principles of religion and the nature of man, we should be in despair, because of sin and the righteous judgment of God. It was not merely general principles of religion that he was interested in. It was one thing that had happened – one thing that God did – that put a new face upon the world. Paul begins the Epistle, therefore, with the things that are 'most in dispute': 'Concerning his Son Jesus Christ our Lord, which was made of the seed of David according to the flesh; and declared to be the Son of God with power, according to the spirit of holiness, by the resurrection from the dead.' There is nothing concessive about that. These were just the things which were mostly in dispute, in those times as today. If you go on through the Epistle to the Romans, you will see that if you re-write it in the modern concessive way, taking your confidence from this one thing that Christ did when he offered himself for the sins of men upon the Cross, you will see that this Epistle to the Romans disappears, and so does the rest of the Bible.

Then we come to the first main section of the Epistle beginning with the eighteenth verse of the first chapter: 'For the wrath of God is revealed from heaven against all ungodliness and unrighteousness of men. . . .' Well, of course we will hear nothing of the wrath of God. We have learned in our day, it is said, to 'interpret' God altogether in terms of love, and have gotten rid of all juridical notions about Him, as though He sat upon some awful judgment seat and condemned men in the white heat of His righteous indignation. So there are three chapters of the Epistle to the Romans gone at one swoop. And when we are getting rid of those chapters, we must by the way get rid of a large part of the teaching of Jesus; for the teaching of Jesus is full of the wrath of God. If you want terrible presentations of the wrath of God, turn not to Cotton Mather or to Jonathan Edwards or to Calvin or to Augustine or to Paul; but turn rather to Jesus of Nazareth. It was Jesus who spoke of the outer darkness and the everlasting fire, of the sin that shall not be forgiven either in this world or in that which is to come.

Then we come to that passage at the end of the third chapter: 'But now apart from the law a righteousness of God hath been manifested, being witnessed by the law and the prophets. . . .' A glance at the long pages of the commentaries, it is said, will show that no one ever has fully understood what those puzzling ten verses mean; and since it is one of the cardinal principles of modern religion that no one shall ever by any chance use his intellect in providing the basis of his religion, it is evident that we shall not have the patience to puzzle those verses out today.

Then of course the fourth chapter of the Epistle to the Romans will have to go, because it is taken up with an appeal to Scripture, and for us the seat of authority in religion is found not in Scripture but in experience.

In the fifth chapter, we may be impressed by the fervour and glow of the language – 'Therefore being justified by faith, we have peace with God through our Lord Jesus Christ . . .' – but after all, it is said, Paul is here operating with theological conceptions of which we can make little.

In the sixth chapter, it is said, we have an interesting phenomenon. At the beginning of the chapter there is presented a supernaturalistic or magical notion of salvation of which we can make nothing; salvation is presented as an act of God and God alone. It is what Paul calls elsewhere the new creation, and what Jesus in the third chapter of John calls the new birth. We moderns, it is said, can make nothing of that. How often is it heard in pulpits today? But then here is the curious phenomenon – after just saying that Christians are dead to sin, and have an entirely new life in Christ, Paul proceeds to urge them not to sin but rather to yield their members as servants to righteousness. Thus, after all, he does appeal to the human will; and so, it is said, we have here a modern and truly ethical notion of salvation struggling to the surface from beneath the magical and supernaturalistic theory of the new creation or the new birth.

Now any one who has any real knowledge of the Bible realises that there is really no contradiction here at all. Certainly a man cannot contribute to his new birth; he has no more part in producing it than he had in producing the natural birth by which he came into this world. But when a man *is* born, he shows that he has been born by proceeding to act. So it is with the new birth. When we were born again, we were born not as full-grown Christian men, but as babes in Christ; and after we have thus been born again we must grow up into Christian manhood. Before we were born again, we could do nothing to please God; we were dead in trespasses and sins. But after we were begotten again by an act of God, after we have thus been made alive by Him, we ought to show that we are alive by being able to act. Thus regeneration or the new birth is followed by the daily battle of the redeemed man against sin. To regeneration or the new birth we could contribute nothing, but in sanctification the man who has been begotten again by God does show that he is spiritually alive by co-operating with God's Spirit. There is a wonderful symmetry and coherence about the teaching of Holy Scripture. But men nowadays have no patience to attend to that coherence, and so the sixth chapter of the Epistle to the Romans, with its doctrine of the new birth, of course will have to go.

In the seventh chapter, it is admitted, we have an interesting human document, that moving account of the struggle between the good and the evil that is in a man. A man, says Paul, consents to the law of God in his inner man, but there is something within him that drags him down. It must be admitted that there is considerable psychological insight in that chapter. But after all, it is said, Paul's experience was peculiar.

There was a sudden break in his life, on the road to Damascus, and so he was inclined to see good and evil in too sharply contrasting colours to suit most of us. That seventh chapter of Romans, interesting though it is, seems to us moderns to be decidedly over-wrought.

When we come to the eighth chapter of Romans, there is no man so modern, I suppose, if he has retained any appreciation for what is fine and noble in literature, as not to feel a certain reverence for those words. Certainly if he is possessed of any human sympathy his reverence for the eighth chapter of Romans will be increased. How often during the past nineteen hundred years when some true saint of God – not some great sinner, but a man who has spent his whole life in pure and unselfish service of his fellow-men – has been asked in the last hour of his life what chapter of the Bible he would like to have read to him, how often such a saint of God, instead of calling for the Sermon on the Mount or any of the ethical parts of the Bible, has said rather: 'Read me the eighth chapter of the Epistle to the Romans.' I tell you, my friends, that chapter is hallowed by tears of joy. 'No condemnation'. 'It is God that justifieth, who is he that condemneth? It is Christ that died, yea rather, that is risen again, who is even at the right hand of God, who also maketh intercession for us.' Ah, my friends, those are the things, rather than any appeal to the rewards of human goodness, that are turned to by the real saints when in the last hour of their lives they are prepared to meet God. A man must be very cold and heartless not to feel a certain reverence for a chapter like that. But after all, people say, even in the eighth chapter of Romans Paul is operating with theological conceptions that we can make little of, and before we can use that chapter we must at least translate it into the thought-forms of the present day. So we proceed to translate it. But the sad thing is that after we get it nicely translated into the thought-forms of the present day, all the glory and the power of it somehow seem to be gone.

With regard to the ninth to the eleventh chapters of Romans, the chapters that contain Paul's philosophy of history – well, man is written entirely too small and God is written entirely too large to suit men nowadays. Those chapters, with their doctrine of predestination and all that, are perhaps the worst in the Epistle; they will certainly have to go.

We have here indeed at last something that is very modern – patriotism. 'I could wish,' Paul says, 'that myself were accursed from Christ for my brethren, my kinsmen according to the flesh.' That is certainly patriotism, and if it had come to going bravely over the top for his country, Paul might have been there with the best of them. It is rather interesting that the apostle Paul, who is the great representative of an individualistic notion of salvation, here gives the most stupendous expression to solidarity of racial feeling. Today an individualistic notion of salvation is altogether despised. This old notion of saving souls, men say, is such a selfish thing. The Y.M.C.A. secretary used to sit at his desk, and possibly now and then had the privilege of leading some lost soul to the Saviour, so that at the sight of the cross, the burden of sin fell into a deep ditch beside the road, and the man went with a new lightness on his way. But now people say that it is a very selfish thing – this trying to save individual men when hosts of others are supposed to be entering into final perdition. People say, 'We would be glad to enter into hell, if anybody is going to enter into hell; we should prefer that to a heaven that is selfish.' It is rather an interesting thing to see that Paul says somewhat the same thing. Only, there is one huge difference: When modern men talk about being perfectly willing to enter hell for others they do not believe in hell, so it means absolutely nothing; but Paul did believe in it and yet he said the same thing.

With the twelfth chapter of the Epistle you enter into what is called the 'practical' part of the letter. People sometimes breathe a sigh of relief when they come to the twelfth chapter of Romans. The troublesome doctrinal part, they say, is at last finished and here at last we have useful hints for daily living. But when you look a little closer, you discover to your consternation, that you have not really escaped from doctrine at all. You discover when you look a little deeper into these practical parts of the New Testament that they are founded upon what people call theology and the new life that comes when a man dies with Christ in order to rise with him. This is not a way of life that is possible for men everywhere, whether Christian or non-Christian. Paul was not foolish enough to think that this type of life is practicable for men who have not been born again. So the 'practical' part of the Epistle is founded altogether upon the doctrine that has been set forth in the first eight chapters. And the discontent of the modern man springs up again. The beginning of that practical section of the Epistle is particularly unfortunate from the modern concessive point of view. Paul says: 'I beseech you, therefore, brethren, by the mercies of God that you present your bodies a living sacrifice.' The 'mercies of God' from the modern point of view will have to go, because the mercies of God that Paul speaks of are the redeeming work of Christ set forth in the 'doctrinal' part of the letter.

Thus when the Epistle to the Romans is re-written in this modern, concessive, non-controversial, non-doctrinal fashion the actual Epistle to the Romans that we have here in our Bibles disappears from beginning to end. But what is the difference between these two Epistles to the Romans – this modern concessive, non-doctrinal, 'tolerant' Epistle on the one hand, and the Epistle that we have in our Bibles on the other? I will tell you in a word what the difference is. The modern, non-controversial Epistle is just the expression of an abysmal scepticism; for if all creeds, despite the fact that they are contradictory to one another, are all equally good, then it follows that they are all equally false or at least all equally uncertain; and if we hold that the doctrine that we now enunciate is merely the setting forth in the thought-forms of this generation of a religious experience that must be set forth in another generation in thought-forms contradictory to these, then it follows that we do not hold the creed that we now set up to be true even here and now. While a thing that is useful now may cease to be useful in another generation, a thing that is true now will remain true beyond the end of time. What is really meant by this non-doctrinal, non-controversial religion is that we have given up the search for truth altogether; we have given up the grounding of our life upon anything that is permanently and objectively true. Such is the modern Epistle to the Romans. It is the expression of a bottomless scepticism. The actual Epistle to the Romans, on the other hand, the Epistle that we have here in our Bibles, in which a man stakes his all upon the truth of one message – that is the expression of a triumphant faith.

As between these two Epistles to the Romans I for my part think we ought to choose the one that Paul wrote. I think that we have no reason to be ashamed of the gospel of Christ. We have less excuse for being ashamed of that gospel today than we had fifty or twenty-five years ago; for the emptiness of a world without that gospel is becoming increasingly plain. There was a time twenty-five or fifty years ago when to a superficial observer it might have seemed as though the Christian life could be continued after Christian doctrine had been given up; a mild 'Liberalism' might have seemed to be full of promise. But that time has gone by. Today it is becoming increasingly evident that we are living over the abyss. What a drab thing, as well as what an alarming thing, is this modern mechanistic age! Well may we turn from such slavery to the glorious liberty of the gospel of Christ. We have no real reason, my friends, to be ashamed of the gospel of Christ.

# 12: *The Separateness of the Church*

*'Ye are the salt of the earth: but if the salt have lost his savour, wherewith shall it be salted? it is thenceforth good for nothing, but to be cast out, and to be trodden under foot of men'* (Matt. 5:13).

IN these words our Lord established at the very beginning the distinctness and separateness of the church. If the sharp distinction is ever broken down between the church and the world, then the power of the church is gone. The church then becomes like salt that has lost its savour, and is fit only to be cast out and to be trodden under foot of men.

It is a great principle, and there never has been a time in all the centuries of Christian history when it has not had to be taken to heart. The really serious attack upon Christianity has not been the attack carried on by fire and sword, by the threat of bonds or death, but it has been the more subtle attack that has been masked by friendly words; it has been not the attack from without but the attack from within. The enemy has done his deadliest work when he has come with words of love and compromise and peace. And how persistent the attack has been! Never in the centuries of the church's life has it been altogether relaxed; always there has been the deadly chemical process, by which, if it had been unchecked, the precious salt would have been merged with the insipidity of the world, and would have been thenceforth good for nothing but to be cast out and to be trodden under foot of men.

The process began at the very beginning in the days when our Lord still walked the Galilean hills. There were many in those days who heard Him gladly: He enjoyed at first the favour of the people. But in that favour He saw a deadly peril; He would have nothing of a half-discipleship that meant the merging of the company of His disciples with the world. How ruthlessly He checked a sentimental enthusiasm! 'Let the dead bury their dead,' He told the enthusiast who came eagerly to Him but was not willing at once to forsake all. 'One thing thou lackest,' He said to the rich young ruler, and the young man went sorrowful away. Truly Jesus did not make it easy to be a follower of Him. 'He that is not with me,' He said, 'is against me.' 'If any man come to me, and hate not his father, and mother, and wife and children . . ., he cannot be my disciple.' How serious a thing it was in those days to stand for Christ!

And it was a serious thing not only in the sphere of conduct but also in the sphere of thought. There could be no greater mistake than to suppose that a man in those days could think as he liked and still be a follower of Jesus. On the contrary the offence lay just as much in the sphere of doctrine as in the sphere of life. There were 'hard sayings,' then as now, to be accepted by the disciples of Jesus, as well as hard commands. 'I am the bread which came down from heaven,' said Jesus. It was indeed a hard saying. No wonder the Jews murmured at Him. 'Is not this Jesus,' they said, 'the son of Joseph, whose father and mother we know? how is it then that he saith, I came down from heaven.' 'How can this man give us his flesh to eat?' Jesus did not make the thing easy for these murmurers. 'Then Jesus said unto them, Verily, verily, I say unto you, Except ye eat the flesh of the Son of man and drink his blood, ye have no life in you.' At that many even of His disciples were offended. 'This is a hard saying,' they said; 'who can hear it?' And so they left Him. 'From that time many of his disciples went back and walked no more with him.' Many of them went back – but not all. 'Then said Jesus unto the twelve, Will ye also go away? Then Simon Peter answered him, Lord, to whom shall we go? thou hast the words of eternal life.' Thus was the precious salt preserved.

Then came the gathering clouds, and finally the cross. In the hour of His agony they all left Him and fled; apparently the movement that He had initiated was hopelessly dead. But such was not the will of God. The disciples were sifted, but there was still something left. Peter was forgiven; the disciples saw the risen Lord; the salt was still preserved.

One hundred and twenty persons were gathered in Jerusalem. It was not a large company; but salt, if it truly have its savour, can permeate the whole lump. The Spirit came in accordance with our Lord's promise, and Peter preached the first sermon in the Christian church. It was hardly a concessive sermon. 'Him being delivered by the determinate counsel and foreknowledge of God, ye have taken, and by wicked hands have crucified and slain.' How unkind Peter was! But by that merciful unkindness they were pricked in their hearts, and three thousand souls were saved.

So there stood the first Christian church in the midst of a hostile world. At first sight it might have seemed to be a mere Jewish sect; the disciples continued to attend the temple services and to lead the life of Jews. But in reality that little company was as separate as if it had been shut off by desert wastes or the wide reaches of the sea; an invisible barrier, to be crossed only by the wonder of the new birth, separated the disciples of Jesus from the surrounding world. 'Of the rest,' we are told, 'durst no man join himself to them.' 'And fear came upon every soul.' So it will always be. When the disciples of Jesus are really faithful to their Lord, they inspire fear; even when Christians are despised and persecuted and harried, they have sometimes made their persecutors secretly afraid. It is not so, indeed, when there is compromise in the Christian camp; it is not so when those who minister in the name of Christ have – as was said in praise some time ago in my hearing of a group of ministers in our day – it is not so when those who minister in the name of Christ 'have their ears to the ground.' But it will be so whenever Christians have their ears, not to the ground, but open only to the voice of God, and when they say simply, in the face of opposition or flattery, as Peter said, 'We must obey God rather than men.'

But after those persecutions, there came in the early church a time of peace – deadly, menacing, deceptive peace, and peace more dangerous by far than the bitterest war. Many of the sect of the Pharisees came into the church – false brethren privily brought in. They were not true Christians, because they trusted in their own works for salvation, and no man can be a Christian who does that. They were not even true adherents of the Old Covenant; for the Old Covenant, despite the Law, was a preparation for the Saviour's coming, and the Law was a school-master unto Christ. Yet they were Christians in name, and they tried to dominate the councils of the church. It was a serious menace; for a moment it looked as though even Peter, true apostle though he was at heart, was being deceived. His principles were right, but by his actions his principles, at Antioch, for one fatal moment, were belied. But it was not God's will that the church should perish; and the man of the hour was there. There was one man who would not consider consequences where a great principle was at stake, who put all personal considerations resolutely aside, and refused to become unfaithful to Christ through any fear of 'splitting the church.' 'When I saw that they walked not uprightly,' said Paul, 'according to the truth of the gospel, I said unto Peter before them all . . .' Thus was the precious salt preserved.

But from another side also the church was menaced by the blandishments of the world; it was menaced not only by a false Judaism, which really meant opposition of man's self-righteousness to the mysterious grace of God, but also by the all-embracing paganism of that day. When the Pauline churches were planted in the cities of the Graeco-Roman world, the battle was not ended but only begun. Would the little spark of new life be kept alive? Certainly it might have seemed to be unlikely in the extreme. The converts were for the most part not men of independent position, but slaves and humble tradesmen; they were bound by a thousand ties to the paganism of their day. How could they possibly avoid being drawn away by the current of the time? The danger certainly was great; and when Paul left an infant church like that at Thessalonica his heart was full of dread.

But God was faithful to His promise, and the first word that came from that infant church was good. The wonder had actually been accomplished; the converts were standing firm; they were in the world but not of the world; their distinctness was kept. In the midst of pagan impurity they were living true Christian lives. But why were they living true Christian lives? That is the really important question. And the answer is plain. They were living Christian lives because they were devoted to Christian truth. 'Ye turned to God,' says Paul, 'from idols to serve the living and true God; and to wait for his Son from heaven, whom he raised from the dead, even Jesus, which delivered us from the wrath to come.' That was the secret of their Christian lives; their Christian lives were founded upon Christian doctrine – upon theism ('the living and true God'), upon Christology ('his Son . . . whom he raised from the dead'), and upon soteriology ('which delivered us from the wrath to come'). They kept the message intact, and hence they lived the life. So it will always be. Lives apparently and superficially Christian can perhaps sometimes be lived by force of habit, without being based upon Christian truth; but that will never do when Christian living, as in pagan Thessalonica, goes against the grain. But in the case of the Thessalonian converts the message was kept intact, and with it the Christian life. Thus again was the precious salt preserved.

The same conflict is observed in more detail in the case of Corinth. What a city Corinth was, to be sure, and how unlikely a place for a Christian church! The address of Paul's First Epistle is, as Bengel says, a mighty paradox. 'To the church of God which is at Corinth' – that was a paradox indeed. And in the First Epistle to the Corinthians we have attested in all its fulness the attempt of paganism, not to combat the church by a frontal attack, but to conquer it by the far deadlier method of merging it gradually and peacefully with the life of the world. Those Corinthian Christians were connected by many ties with the pagan life of their great city. What should they do about clubs and societies; what should they do about invitations to dinners where meat that had been offered to idols was set before the guests? What should they do about marriage and the like? These were practical questions, but they involved the great principle of the distinctness and exclusiveness of the church. Certainly the danger was very great, the converts were in great danger, from the human point of view, of sinking back into the corrupt life of the world.

But the conflict was not merely in the sphere of conduct. More fundamentally it was in the sphere of thought. Paganism in Corinth was far too astute to think that Christian life could be attacked when Christian doctrine remained. And so pagan practice was prompted by an appeal to pagan theory; the enemy engaged in an attempt to sublimate or explain away the fundamental things of the Christian faith. Somewhat after the manner of the Auburn 'Affirmationists' in our day, paganism in the Corinthian church sought to substitute the Greek notion of the immortality of the soul for the Christian doctrine of the resurrection. But God had His witness; the apostle Paul was not deceived; and in a great passage – the most important words, historically, perhaps, that have ever been penned – he reviewed the sheer factual basis of the Christian faith. 'How that Christ died for our sins according to the scriptures; and that he was buried, and that he rose again the third day according to the scriptures.' There is the foundation of the Christian edifice. Paganism was gnawing away – not yet directly, but by ultimate implication – at that foundation in Corinth, as it has been doing so in one way or another ever since. But Paul was there, and many of the five hundred witnesses were still alive. The gospel message was kept distinct, in the Pauline churches, from the wisdom of the world; the precious salt was still preserved.

Then, in the second century, there came another deadly conflict. It was again a conflict not with an enemy without, but with an enemy within. The Gnostics used the name of Christ; they tried to dominate the church; they appealed to the Epistles of Paul. But despite their use of Christian language they were pagan through and through. Modern scholarship, on this point, has tended to confirm the judgment of the great orthodox writers of that day; Gnosticism was at bottom no mere variety of Christian belief, no mere heresy, but paganism masquerading in Christian dress. Many were deceived; the danger was very great. But it was not God's will that the church should perish. Irenaeus was there, and Tertullian with his vehement defence. The church was saved – not by those who cried 'Peace, peace, when there is no peace,' but by zealous contenders for the faith. Again, out of a great danger, the precious salt was preserved.

Time would fail us to speak of Athanasius and of Augustine and the rest, but they too were God's instruments in the preservation of the precious salt. Certainly the attack in those days was subtle enough almost to deceive the very elect. Grant the Semi-Arians their one letter in *homoiousios*, the smallest letter of the Greek alphabet, and Christ would have been degraded to the level of a creature, mythology would have been substituted for the living God, and the victory of paganism would have been complete. From the human point of view the life of the church was hanging by a hair. But God was watching over His own; Athanasius stood against the world; and the precious salt was preserved.

Then came the Middle Ages. How long, and how dark, in some respects, was the time! It is hard to realise that eleven centuries elapsed between Augustine and Luther, yet such was the case. Never in the interval, indeed, was God altogether without His witnesses; the light still shone from the sacred page; but how dim, in that atmosphere, the light seemed to be! The gospel might have seemed to be buried forever. Yet in God's good time it came forth again with new power – the same gospel that Augustine and Paul had proclaimed. What stronger proof could there be that that gospel had come from God? Where in the history of religion is there any parallel for such a revival, after such an interval, and with such a purity of faithfulness to what had formerly been believed? A gospel that survived the Middle Ages will probably, it may well be hoped, never perish from the earth, but will be the word of life unto the end of the world.

Yet in those early years of the sixteenth century how dark was the time! When Luther made his visit to Rome, what did he find – what did he find there in the centre of the Christian world? He found paganism blatant and triumphant and unashamed; he found the glories of ancient Greece come to life in the Italian renaissance, but with those glories the self-sufficiency and the rebellion against God and the moral degradation of the natural man. Apparently paganism had at last won its age-long battle; apparently it had made a clean sweep over the people of God, apparently the church had at last become quite indistinguishable from the world.

But in the midst of the general wreck one thing at least was preserved. Many things were lost, but one thing was still left – the medieval church had never lost the Word of God. The Bible had indeed become a book with seven seals; it had been buried under a mass of misinterpretation never equalled perhaps until the absurdities indulged in by the Modernism of the present day – a mass of misinterpretation which seemed to hide it from the eyes of men. But at last an Augustinian monk penetrated beneath the mass of error, read the Scriptures with his own eyes; and the Reformation was born. Thus again was the precious salt preserved.

Then came Calvin and the great consistent system which he founded upon the Word of God. How glorious were the by-products of that system of revealed truth! A great stream of liberty spread from Geneva throughout Europe and to America across the sea. But if the by-products were glorious, more glorious by far was the truth itself, and the life that it caused men to live. How sweet and beautiful a thing was the life of the Protestant Christian home, where the Bible was the sole guide and stay! Have we really devised a substitute for that life in these latter days? I think not, my friends. There was liberty there, and love, and peace with God.

But the church after the Reformation was not to have any permanent rest, as indeed it is probably not to have rest at any time in this evil world. Still the conflict of the ages went on, and paganism prepared for an assault greater and more insidious perhaps than any that had gone before. At first there was a frontal attack – Voltaire and Rousseau and the Goddess Reason and the terrors of the French Revolution and all that. As will always be the case, such an attack was bound to fail. But the enemy has now changed his method, and the attack is coming, not from without, but, in far more dangerous fashion, from within. During the past one hundred years the Protestant churches of the world have gradually been becoming permeated by paganism in its most insidious form.

Sometimes paganism is blatant, as, for example, in a recent sermon the burden of which was, 'I Believe in Man.' That was the very quintessence of the pagan spirit – confidence in human resources substituted for the Christian consciousness of sin. But what was there blatant is found in subtler forms in many places throughout the church. The Bible, with a complete abandonment of all scientific historical method, and of all common sense, is made to say the exact opposite of what it means; no Gnostic, no medieval monk with his fourfold sense of Scripture, ever produced more absurd Biblical interpretation than can be heard every Sunday in the pulpits of New York. Even prayer in many quarters is made a thinly disguised means of propaganda against the truth of the gospel; men pray that there may be peace, where peace means victory for the enemies of Christ. Thus gradually the church is being permeated by the spirit of the world; it is becoming what the Auburn Affirmationists call an 'inclusive' church; it is becoming salt that has lost its savour and is henceforth good for nothing but to be cast out and to be trodden under foot of men.

At such a time, what should be done by those who love Christ? I think, my friends, that they should at least face the facts; I do not believe that they should bury their heads like ostriches in the sand; I do not think that they should soothe themselves with the minutes of the General Assembly or the reports of the Boards or the imposing rows of figures which the church papers contain. Last week it was reported that the churches of America increased their membership by 690,000. Are you encouraged by these figures? I for my part am not encouraged a bit. I have indeed my own grounds for encouragement, especially those which are found in the great and precious promises of God. But

113

these figures have no place among them. How many of these 690,000 names do you think are really written in the Lamb's book of life? A small proportion, I fear. Church membership today often means nothing more, as has well been said, than a vague admiration for the moral character of Jesus; the church in countless communities is little more than a Rotary Club. One day, as I was walking through a neighbouring city, I saw, not an altar with an inscription to an unknown god, but something that filled me with far more sorrow than that could have done. I saw a church with a large sign on it, which read somewhat like this: 'Not a member? Come in and help us make this a better community.' Truly we have wandered far from the day when entrance into the church involved confession of faith in Christ as the Saviour from sin.

The truth is that in these days the ecclesiastical currency has been sadly debased. Church membership, church office, the ministry, no longer mean what they ought to mean. But what shall we do? I think, my friends, that, cost what it may, we ought at least to face the facts. It will be hard; it will seem impious to timid souls; many will be hurt. But in God's name let us get rid of shams and have reality at least. Let us stop soothing ourselves with columns of statistics, and face the spiritual facts; let us recall this paper currency and get back to a standard of gold.

When we do that, and when we come to God in prayer, with the real facts spread before Him, as Hezekiah spread before Him the letter of the enemy, there will be some things to cheer our hearts. God has not left Himself altogether without His witnesses. Humble they may often be, and despised by the wisdom of the world; but they are not perhaps altogether without the favour of God. In China, in Great Britain, and in America there have been some who have raised their voices bravely for their Saviour and Lord.

True, the forces of unbelief have not yet been checked,

and none can say whether our own American Presbyterian Church, which we love so dearly, will be preserved. It may be that paganism will finally control,
and that Christian men and women may have to
withdraw from a church that has lost its distinctness
from the world. Once in the course of history, at the
beginning of the sixteenth century, that method of
withdrawal was God's method of preserving the precious salt. But it may be also that our Church in its
corporate capacity, in its historic grandeur, may yet
stand for Christ. God grant that it may be so! The
future at any rate is in God's hand, and in some way or
other – let us learn that much from history – the salt
will be preserved.

What are you going to do, my brothers, in this great
time of crisis? What a time it is to be sure! What a time
of glorious opportunity! Will you stand with the world,
will you shrink from controversy, will you witness for
Christ only where witnessing costs nothing, will you
pass through these stirring days without coming to any
real decision? Or will you learn the lesson of Christian
history; will you penetrate, by your study and your
meditation, beneath the surface; will you recognise in
that which prides itself on being modern an enemy that
is as old as the hills; will you hope, and pray, not for a
mere continuance of what now is, but for a rediscovery
of the gospel that can make all things new; will you
have recourse to the charter of Christian liberty in the
Word of God? God grant that some of you may do that!
God grant that some of you, even though you be not
now decided, may come to say, as you go forth into the
world: 'It is hard in these days to be a Christian; the
adversaries are strong; I am weak; but thy Word is true
and thy Spirit will be with me; here am I, Lord, send
me.'

# 13: *Prophets False and True*

*'And Micaiah said, As the Lord liveth, what the Lord saith unto me, that will I speak'* (1 Kings 22:14).

THE text is a great text and it is taken from a great chapter. Some chapters of the Bible are certainly greater than others, and it is by no means derogatory to the authority of Scripture to recognise their special greatness. The doctrine of plenary inspiration does not mean, as its opponents often represent it as meaning, that all parts of the Bible are equally valuable – it only means that all parts of the Bible are equally true. Even the least valuable parts of the Bible have, indeed, their place. Lovers of poetry love the level lines of Shakespeare; so we Christians cherish the great level, prose chapters of the Word of God. Even in the level pathways of Scripture we can walk with God and learn of Him. But then when we have passed through such a stretch in our reading of the Bible, where distant scenes are concealed, suddenly we emerge sometimes as we read, as upon the brow of some hill, and discern before us with wondering eyes a wide, free prospect of the world and destiny and human duty. And there, through the great expanse stretched out before, may be seen a narrow path that leads over hill and dale until in the dim distance it loses itself in the mysterious brightness of the city of God.

Such a great chapter of the Bible, such a Pisgah height of vision, is found in the twenty-second chapter of the First Book of Kings. The two kings sat on their thrones at the gate of Samaria; the armies were marshalled before them for the battle. But before they went forth Jehoshaphat said unto the king of Israel: 'Enquire, I pray thee, at the word of the Lord today.' And the king of Israel gathered the prophets together, about four hundred men, and said unto them: 'Shall I go against Ramoth-Gilead to battle, or shall I forbear?' And they said: 'Go up; for the Lord shall deliver it unto the hand of the king.'

But Jehoshaphat was not satisfied. Why he was not satisfied I do not know. Perhaps it was because of conscience. He was doing that which he knew in his heart of hearts to be wrong – what part had he with the wicked Ahab? Perhaps, as men will do when conscience speaks, he sought ever further confirmation of that thing, really wrong, that he desired to do. Four hundred prophets had spoken, but their hubbub had not quite succeeded in drowning the inner voice. So Jehoshaphat said: 'Is there not here a prophet of the Lord besides, that we might enquire of him?' And Ahab said: 'There is yet one man, Micaiah the son of Imlah, by whom we may enquire of the Lord; but I hate him; for he doth not prophesy good concerning me, but evil.' And Jehoshaphat said, 'Let not the king say so.'

So Micaiah was brought and stood before the king. The messenger who brought him was his friend, and coached him as to what he should say. 'Behold now, the words of the prophets declare good unto the king with one mouth; let thy word, I pray thee, be like the word of one of them, and speak that which is good.' But Micaiah said: 'As the Lord liveth, what the Lord saith unto me, that will I speak.' So he came and stood before the king. And the king said unto him: 'Micaiah, shall we go against Ramoth-Gilead to battle, or shall we forbear?' And he answered him: 'Go and prosper: for the Lord shall deliver it into the hand of the king.'

Do you think that Micaiah was untrue to the word of the Lord that was in him; do you think that he belied the brave words that he had just spoken to the officer who had brought him to the king? Oh no, my friends;

the words of Micaiah were no denial of his sacred trust, but they were the words of a devastating scorn. 'I will give you,' he said in effect, 'the only prophecy that you deserve, the prophecy of a parrot that speaks only what others speak, the prophecy of a courtier who speaks only what will win the favour of men. Go and prosper: for the Lord shall deliver it into the hand of the king.' Ahab agreed with our exegesis; Ahab knew well enough that he was being mocked. 'How many times shall I adjure thee,' he said, 'that thou tell me nothing but that which is true in the name of the Lord?'

And then came a surprising thing; then came, when it was least to be expected, in that unfavourable atmosphere, a true word of the Lord. Even in form it was quite different from the words that had gone before. There was no more parrot-like repetition of optimistic words; there was no more vulgar shoving of imaginary Syrians with horns of iron. Instead, in the answer of Micaiah, we suddenly find ourselves in the region of high poetry where the great prophets move. 'I saw all Israel,' said Micaiah, 'scattered upon the hills, as sheep that have not a shepherd, and the Lord said, These have no master, let them return every man to his house in peace.'

The rest of the story is quickly told. The word of the Lord was unheeded; Micaiah went back to partake of the bread of affliction and the water of affliction; the kings went up into the battle; and the dogs soon licked the blood of Ahab by the pool of Samaria. Which kind of prophets will you be as you go out from this place? Will you be like Zedekiah the son of Chenaanah, pushing imaginary Syrians with horns of iron, speaking the word that others are speaking, speaking the word that men want you to speak? Or will you be prophets after the order of Micaiah?

In one sense, I admit, you cannot be prophets at all. A prophet was a man to whom God had directly spoken, who appealed to no external authority, but said simply,

'Thus saith the Lord.' There are those who claim to be such prophets today. But few of us, I think, will be inclined to accept their claims. True prophecy, in the supernatural, biblical sense does not exist today; like other miracles it has ceased. Why it has ceased we may not perhaps be able to say; the ways of God with men in the Christian religion constitute not a scheme that we can work out according to principles of our own, but, as Chesterton says, for us at least, a story, a romance, full of strange, unexpected things. Perhaps, indeed, we may see a little way at this point into the purposes of God, we may perhaps understand a little of the reason why prophecy has ceased. There is a wonderful completeness in the revelation that the Bible contains. We have in the Bible an account of the great presuppositions that should underlie all our thinking – the righteousness and holiness of God and the sinfulness of man. And then we have an account of the way in which God saved man once for all by the redeeming work of Christ. That redeeming work was not partial but complete. It needs to be applied, indeed, by the Holy Spirit; but the redemption that is to be applied was accomplished once for all by Christ. It is hard to see, therefore, what need there is of supernatural revelation until that great day when the Lord shall come again to usher in His kingdom in final power.

But although no fresh supernatural revelation is given in the present age, it would be a great mistake to disparage the dispensation under which we are living. That dispensation is the dispensation of the Holy Spirit: even the absence of new revelations is itself in one sense a mark of glory; it is an indication of the wondrous completeness of God's initial gift to His church. In Old Testament times there was prophecy, because then God's redemptive plan was still in the process of unfolding; but we are the heirs of the ages and have the Saviour Himself. Only one great act remains in the drama of redemption – the mighty catastrophic coming of our Lord in glory.

Meanwhile we have the Holy Spirit, and we have the Scripture of the Old and New Testaments that the Holy Spirit uses. Much mischief has been wrought in the church by false notions of 'the witness of the Spirit'; it has sometimes been supposed that the Holy Spirit makes us independent of the Bible. Just the opposite is the case. The Holy Spirit is the Spirit of truth. He does not contradict in one generation what He has said in another. He does not contradict the Scriptures that He himself has given. On the contrary, what He really does is to make the words of Scripture glow with a heavenly light and burn in the hearts of men. Those Scriptures are placed in your hands. You may not say with the prophets of old: 'God has spoken directly and independently to me; I appeal to no external authority; when I speak it is "Thus saith the Lord."' But you can do something else. You can mount your pulpit stairs; open reverently the Bible on the desk; pray to the gracious Spirit to make plain the words that He has spoken; and so unfold to needy people the Word of God.

Do you think that that is a low function? Do you think that it involves a slavish kind of dependence on a book? Do you think that it means that advance and freedom are to be checked? The history of the church should be the answer. Again and again history has shown that the Bible, when accepted in the very highest sense as the Word of God, does not stifle life but gives life birth; does not enslave men, but sets them free. Those who talk about emancipating themselves from the slavish doctrine of what they call 'verbal' inspiration are not really emancipating themselves from a tyranny, but they are tearing up the charter upon which all human liberty depends.

And so, after all, you can say in a high, true sense, as you draw upon the rich store of revelation in the Bible: 'Thus saith the Lord.' If you accept the Bible as the

Word of God you will have one qualification of a preacher. Whatever be the limitations of your gifts, you will at least have a message. You will be, in one respect at least, unlike most persons who love to talk in public at the present time; you will have one qualification of a speaker – you will at least have something to say. But what is it that you will have to say? What will be the kind of message that God has given you to proclaim?

In the first place, it will unquestionably be a message of warning; you will be called upon to tell men of evil that is to come. That will no doubt make you unpopular. Men like encouragement; they like to be told, with regard to the Ramoth-Gilead of their pet projects, to go up and prosper, for the Lord will deliver it into the hand of the king; they do not like to see gloomy visions of all Israel scattered upon the hills as sheep that have not a shepherd. It is not Micaiah the son of Imlah but Zedekiah the son of Chenaanah that often has the favour of the crowd.

I am going to venture, however, to say a brief word in defence of pessimism. There are times when pessimism is a very encouraging thing. Last summer I took a voyage down the New England coast one foggy afternoon and night; it was one of the thickest nights that I have ever seen even on those fog-bound waters. Now I am glad to say that the captain of each of the two boats on which I travelled was a thorough pessimist. For a time the boat would plough along at full speed; but then, for no apparent reason, she would stop and rock quietly upon the gentle swells, and then proceed at a snail's pace. Presently the mournful sound of a buoy would be heard and then the buoy would come into sight. The buoys were usually exactly where the captain expected them to be; but unless he saw them he took a thoroughly pessimistic view as to their whereabouts. The result of such pessimism was good. The sound of the fog-horn was, indeed, lugubrious and

121

hardly conducive to repose; but at least we got safely into Boston in the morning.

There are ship-captains who are less pessimistic than the captain of that boat. Such an one, for example, was the captain of the ill-fated *Titanic*. He hoped that all was well, and kept the engines going at full speed. I am certainly not presuming to blame him. Perhaps every captain not gifted with superhuman vision would have been as optimistic as he. But, whether excusably or not, optimistic he certainly was; and his optimism was fatal to many hundreds of human lives. The great ship ploughed onward through the night; and now she lies at the bottom of the sea. Oh, that no mere weak mortal but some true prophet of God had been upon the bridge that night!

That disaster is a figure of what will come of optimism in the churches of today. Superficially our ecclesiastical life seems to be progressing as it always did: the cabins are full of comfortable passengers; the orchestra is playing a lively air; the rows of lighted windows shine cheerfully out into the night. But all the time death is lurking beneath. In this time of deadly peril there are leaders who say that all is well; there are leaders who decry controversy and urge peace, declaring that the church is all perfectly loyal and true. God forgive them, brethren! I say it with all my heart: may God forgive them for the evil that they are doing to Christ's little ones: may the Holy Spirit open their eyes while yet there is time! Meanwhile, in the case of many of the churches, the great ship rushes onward to the risk, at least, of doom.

Yes, my friends, if you be true prophets like Micaiah, you will be called upon to warn the church. But you will also be called upon to warn individual men and women. And the thing about which you will be called upon to warn them is sin. In warning men of sin you will of course often have to cast popularity aside. Like some good physicians, you will be laughed at as alarmists and hated as those who take the pleasure out of life. Men love to be encouraged by false hopes; the world is full of quack remedies for sin. In this spiritual sphere, moreover, there is no protection against quacks; there is no paternalistic state legislature to regulate medical practice and protect the unwary from their fate. In such a world of quackery and of false optimism you will have to come forward with your terrible diagnosis of sin.

You will come, indeed, not merely with a diagnosis but also with a cure. Only, the cure is no light, merely palliative, thing, but one that enters into the very depths:

> *There is a fountain filled with blood*
> *Drawn from Emmanuel's veins;*
> *And sinners plunged beneath that flood,*
> *Lose all their guilty stains.*

I am perfectly well aware that many men do not like that hymn; it offends their sensibilities; they are omitting it, I believe, from their hymn-books. Now I am perfectly ready to confess that I myself do not like it so much as I do some other hymns. Possibly its imagery is too bold and too fully carried out; possibly it spreads a little too unreservedly in the light of day what would better remain hidden in the depths of the Christian heart. I do not know. I prefer to it, I think, that hymn of Isaac Watts:

> *When I survey the wondrous cross*
> *On which the Prince of glory died,*
> *My richest gain I count but loss,*
> *And pour contempt on all my pride.*

And if I want bold imagery I turn to the original fourth verse of that hymn.

> *His dying crimson like a robe.*
> *Spreads o'er His body on the tree.*

*Then am I dead to all the globe,*
*And all the globe is dead to me.*

I quite agree with Matthew Arnold in holding that that hymn is the greatest of all those hymns that go to the depths in presenting the remedy for sin.

There are those, I know, who tell us that we ought not to place such emphasis upon the cross. They talk to us – these men who belittle the cross of Christ, these men who trouble its divine simplicity with the wisdom, or rather the folly, of this world – they talk to us about having a living Christ and not a dead Christ. Well, my friends, I think we certainly ought to have a living Christ. Without a sweet, intimate communion with Him there is no Christian experience; without service of Him as a present Companion and Helper and Judge, as we go about our labours from day to day, there is no Christian life. Yes, we certainly ought to have a living Christ. But let us never forget one thing – that living Christ with whom we have communion bore in His hands the print of the nails. Oh, no, my friends; only at the foot of the cross is there a remedy for sin; there only is peace, there only do we find our first communion with the Christ with whom then we shall live forevermore.

Certainly if you preach this gospel of the cross, you will have to bear reproach. If you preach this gospel faithfully, you will see men whom you have called your friends, men whom you have served in the hour of need, turn against you and join the general hue and cry; you will be subjected to misrepresentation and slander of all kinds; you will bear both ridicule and abuse; you will be attacked behind and before. But there are some compensations in the prophet's life. Many will speak of you; but there is One who will say: 'Well done, good and faithful servant.'

Men sometimes think that the day of Christian heroism is over. I do not believe it. There may come, sooner than we think, even physical persecutions. Around us there is slowly closing in the tyranny of a democratic collectivism which is far more inimical to liberty of conscience than the comparatively ineffective despotisms of the past. But however that may be, even now you will be called upon to endure hardness for the cross of Christ. You will face in subtle forms the age-long temptation to mitigate the exclusiveness of the gospel – to preach it as one way of salvation without denying that other ways may lead to the same end, to make your preaching, as Satan persuasively puts it, 'positive and not negative,' to be 'tolerant of opposing views,' to work contentedly in the church with those who reject the cross of Christ, to preach Christ boldly in your pulpit (where preaching Him may cost you nothing) and then deny Him by your vote in church councils and courts. But God grant that you may resist the Tempter's voice; God save you from the sin of paring down the gospel to suit the pride of men; God grant that you may deliver your message straight and full and plain. Only so, whatever else you may sacrifice, will you have one thing – the favour of the Lord Jesus Christ.

And only so will you be the instrument in saving souls. Do you think men's souls are satisfied by the current preaching of the day, with its encouragement of human pride? It might seem so. The churches are crowded where Zedekiah the son of Chenaanah and his associates hold forth; one can sometimes in those churches scarcely obtain a seat; hundreds are turned away at the doors. But let us not be deceived by appearances. Among those crowds – contented though they may seem to a superficial observer to be – there are many hungry hearts. Despite all the apparent satisfaction of the world with this 'other gospel' of a non-doctrinal Christianity, this 'other gospel' that is dictated by human pride, there is deep down in the human heart a hunger for the Word of God. Despite all the efforts of modern prophets, all that Zedekiah and his far more than four hundred associates can do, despite the hubbub of modern optimism, you will find, here and there at least, in this modern world, listening to these modern preachers, those who say, after listening to it all: 'Is there not here a prophet of the Lord besides that we might enquire of him?'

And then, when you find such persons, you will have your chance; then, while angels look on, you will have your moment of glorious opportunity – the moment when you can speak the word that God has given you to speak. It will be a word of warning; false hopes must be ruthlessly destroyed. But it will also be a word of wondrous joy. What can be compared, brethren, to the privilege of proclaiming to needy souls the exuberant joy of the gospel of Christ? Can all the plaudits of the world, the false reputation of breadth and tolerance, and praise of those who know not Christ? I think not, my brethren. I think that those things, when we come to face the great issues of life and death, will seem more worthless than the dust of the streets. There is one thing and one thing only that is worth while; it is to be faithful to Him who loved us and gave Himself for us; it is to be faithful to Him who is Judge and Ruler of all, and to speak His word for the salvation of dying men.

Pray God that you, whom we have come during your stay here to know and love, may be thus faithful; pray God that you may be true prophets after the order of Micaiah; pray God that you may say to those who would persuasively turn you aside from your true calling, who would urge you to trust in human influences for the success of your labours, who would urge you to speak the words that others speak, who would say: 'Behold now, the words of the prophets declare good unto the king with one mouth; let thy word, I pray thee, be like the word of one of them, and speak that which is good' – pray God that you may say to them, with Micaiah, after you have been at the foot of the cross: 'As the Lord liveth, what the Lord saith unto me, that will I speak.'

# 14: *The Good Fight of Faith*

*'And the peace of God, which passeth all understanding, shall keep your hearts and minds through Christ Jesus'* (Phil. 4:7). *'Fight the good fight of faith'* (I Tim. 6:12 [part] ).

THE Apostle Paul was a great fighter. His fighting was partly against external enemies – against hardships of all kinds. Five times he was scourged by the Jews, three times by the Romans; he suffered shipwreck four times; and was in perils of waters, in perils of robbers, in perils by his own countrymen, in perils by the heathen, in perils in the city, in perils in the wilderness, in perils in the sea, in perils among false brethren. And finally he came to the logical end of such a life, by the headsman's axe. It was hardly a peaceful life, but was rather a life of wild adventure. Lindbergh, I suppose, got a thrill when he hopped off to Paris, and people are in search of thrills to-day; but if you wanted a really unbroken succession of thrills, I think you could hardly do better than try knocking around the Roman Empire of the first century with the Apostle Paul, engaged in the unpopular business of turning the world upside down.

But these physical hardships were not the chief battle in which Paul was engaged. Far more trying was the battle that he fought against enemies in his own camp. Everywhere his rear was threatened by an all-engulfing paganism or by a perverted Judaism that had missed the real purpose of the Old Testament law. Read the Epistles with care, and you see Paul always in conflict. At one time he fights paganism in life, the notion that all kinds of conduct are lawful to the

Christian man, a philosophy that makes Christian liberty a mere aid to pagan licence. At another time, he fights paganism in thought, the sublimation of the Christian doctrine of the resurrection of the body into the pagan doctrine of the immortality of the soul. At still another time, he fights the effort of human pride to substitute man's merit, as the means of salvation, for divine grace; he fights the subtle propaganda of the Judaisers with its misleading appeal to the Word of God. Everywhere we see the great apostle in conflict for the preservation of the church. It is as though a mighty flood were seeking to engulf the church's life; dam the break at one point in the levee, and another break appears somewhere else. Everywhere paganism was seeping through; not for one moment did Paul have peace; always he was called upon to fight.

Fortunately, he was a true fighter; and by God's grace he not only fought, but he won. At first sight, indeed, he might have seemed to have lost. The lofty doctrine of divine grace, the centre and core of the gospel that Paul preached, did not always dominate the mind and heart of the subsequent church. The Christianity of the Apostolic Fathers, of the Apologists, of Irenæus, is very different from the Christianity of Paul. The church meant to be faithful to the apostle; but the pure doctrine of the cross runs counter to the natural man, and not always, even in the church, was it fully understood. Read the Epistle to the Romans first, and then read Irenæus, and you are conscious of a mighty decline. No longer does the gospel stand out sharp and clear; there is a large admixture of human error; and it might seem as though Christian freedom, after all, was to be entangled in the meshes of a new law.

But even Irenæus is very different from the Judaisers; something had been gained even in his day: and God had greater things than Irenæus in store for the church. The Epistles which Paul struck forth in conflict with the opponents in his own day remained in the New

Testament as a perennial source of life for the people of God. Augustine, on the basis of the Epistles, set forth the Pauline doctrine of sin and grace; and then, after centuries of compromise with the natural man, the Reformation rediscovered the great liberating Pauline doctrine of justification by faith. So it has always been with Paul. Just when he seems to be defeated, his greatest triumphs, by God's grace, are in store.

The human instruments, however, which God uses in those triumphs are no pacifists, but great fighters like Paul himself. Little affinity for the great apostle has the whole tribe of the considerers of consequences, the whole tribe of the compromisers ancient and modern. The real companions of Paul are the great heroes of the faith. But who are those heroes? Are they not true fighters, one and all? Tertullian fought a mighty battle against Marcion; Athanasius fought against the Arians; Augustine fought against Pelagius; and as for Luther, he fought a brave battle against kings and princes and popes for the liberty of the people of God. Luther was a great fighter; and we love him for it. So was Calvin; so were John Knox and all the rest. It is impossible to be a true soldier of Jesus Christ and not fight.

God grant that you – students in this seminary – may be fighters, too! Probably you have your battles even now: you have to contend against sins gross or sins refined; you have to contend against the sin of slothfulness and inertia; you have, many of you, I know very well, a mighty battle on your hands against doubt and despair. Do not think it strange if you fall thus into divers temptations. The Christian life is a warfare after all. John Bunyan rightly set it forth under the allegory of a Holy War; and when he set it forth, in his greater book, under the figure of a pilgrimage, the pilgrimage, too, was full of battles. There are, indeed, places of refreshment on the Christian way; the House Beautiful was provided by the King at the top of the Hill

Difficulty, for the entertainment of pilgrims, and from the Delectable Mountains could sometimes be discerned the shining towers of the City of God. But just after the descent from the House Beautiful, there was the battle with Apollyon, and the Valley of Humiliation, and later came the Valley of the Shadow of Death. Yes, the Christian faces a mighty conflict in this world. Pray God that in that conflict you may be true men; good soldiers of Jesus Christ, not willing to compromise with your great enemy, not easily cast down, and seeking ever the renewing of your strength in the Word and sacraments and prayer!

You will have a battle, too, when you go forth as ministers into the church. The church is now in a period of deadly conflict. The redemptive religion known as Christianity is contending, in our own church and in all the larger churches of the world, against a totally alien type of religion. As always, the enemy conceals his most dangerous assaults under pious phrases and half truths. The shibboleths of the adversary have sometimes a very deceptive sound. 'Let us propagate Christianity,' the adversary says, 'but let us not always be engaged in arguing in defence of it; let us make our preaching positive, and not negative; let us avoid controversy; let us hold to a Person and not to a dogma; let us sink small doctrinal differences and seek the unity of the church of Christ; let us drop doctrinal accretions and interpret Christ for ourselves; let us look for our knowledge of Christ, not to ancient books, but to the living Christ in our hearts; let us not impose Western creeds on the Eastern mind; let us be tolerant of opposing views.' Such are some of the shibboleths of that agnostic Modernism which is the deadliest enemy of the Christian religion to-day. They deceive some of God's people some of the time; they are heard sometimes from the lips of good Christian people, who have not the slightest inkling of what they mean. But their true meaning, to thinking men, is becoming increasingly

131

clear. Increasingly it is becoming necessary for a man to decide whether he is going to stand or not to stand for the Lord Jesus Christ as he is presented to us in the Word of God.

If you decide to stand for Christ, you will not have an easy life in the ministry. Of course, you may try to evade the conflict. All men will speak well of you if, after preaching no matter how unpopular a gospel on Sunday, you will only vote against that gospel in the councils of the church the next day; you will graciously be permitted to believe in supernatural Christianity all you please if you will only act as though you did not believe in it, if you will only make common cause with its opponents. Such is the programme that will win the favour of the church. A man may believe what he pleases, provided he does not believe anything strongly enough to risk his life on it and fight for it. 'Tolerance' is the great word. Men even ask for tolerance when they look to God in prayer. But how can any Christian possibly pray such a prayer as that? What a terrible prayer it is, how full of disloyalty to the Lord Jesus Christ! There is a sense, of course, in which tolerance is a virtue. If by it you mean tolerance on the part of the State, that forbearance of majorities toward minorities, the resolute rejection of any measures of physical compulsion in propagating either what is true or what is false, then of course the Christian ought to favour tolerance with all his might and main, and ought to lament the widespread growth of intolerance in America to-day. Or if you mean by tolerance forbearance toward personal attacks upon yourself, or courtesy and patience and fairness in dealing with all errors of whatever kind, then again tolerance is a virtue. But to pray for tolerance apart from such qualifications, in particular to pray for tolerance without careful definition of that of which you are to be tolerant, is just to pray for the breakdown of the Christian religion; for the Christian religion is intolerant to the core. There lies the whole offence of the cross – and also the whole power of it. Always the gospel would have been received with favour by the world if it had been presented merely as one way of salvation; the offence came because it was presented as the only way, and because it made relentless war upon all other ways. God save us, then, from this 'tolerance' of which we hear so much! God deliver us from the sin of making common cause with those who deny or ignore the blessed gospel of Jesus Christ! God save us from the deadly guilt of consenting to the presence as our representatives in the church of those who lead Christ's little ones astray; God make us, whatever else we are, just faithful messengers, who present, without fear or favour, not our word, but the Word of God!

But if you are such messengers, you will have the opposition, not only of the world, but increasingly, I fear, of the church. I cannot tell you that your sacrifice will be light. No doubt it would be noble to care nothing whatever about the judgment of our fellowmen. But to such nobility I confess that I for my part have not quite attained, and I cannot expect you to have attained to it. I confess that academic preferments, easy access to great libraries, the society of cultured people, in general the thousand advantages that come from being regarded as respectable people in a respectable world – I confess that these things seem to me to be in themselves good and desirable things. Yet the servant of Jesus Christ, to an increasing extent, is being obliged to give them up. Certainly, in making that sacrifice we do not complain; for we have something with which all that we have lost is not worthy to be compared. Still, it can hardly be said that any unworthy motives of self-interest can lead us to adopt a course which brings us nothing but reproach. Where, then, shall we find a sufficient motive for such a course as that; where shall we find courage to stand against the whole current of the age; where shall we find courage for this fight of faith? I do not think that we shall obtain courage by any mere lust of conflict. In some battles that means may perhaps suffice. Soldiers in bayonet practice were sometimes, and for all I know still are, taught to give a shout when they thrust their bayonets at imaginary enemies; I heard them doing it even long after the armistice in France. That serves, I suppose, to overcome the natural inhibition of civilised man against sticking a knife into human bodies. It is thought to develop the proper spirit of conflict. Perhaps it may be necessary in some kinds of war. But it will hardly serve in this Christian conflict. In this conflict I do not think we can be good fighters simply by being resolved to fight. For this battle is a battle of love; and nothing ruins a man's service in it so much as a spirit of hate.

No, if we want to learn the secret of this warfare, we shall have to look deeper; and we can hardly do better than turn again to that great fighter, the Apostle Paul. What was the secret of his power in the mighty conflict; how did he learn to fight?

The answer is paradoxical; but it is very simple. Paul was a great fighter because he was at peace. He who said, 'Fight the good fight of faith,' spoke also of 'the peace of God which passeth all understanding'; and in that peace the sinews of his war were found. He fought against the enemies that were without because he was at peace within; there was an inner sanctuary in his life that no enemy could disturb. There, my friends, is the great central truth. You cannot fight successfully with beasts, as Paul did at Ephesus; you cannot fight successfully against evil men, or against the devil and his spiritual powers of wickedness in high places, unless when you fight against those enemies there is One with whom you are at peace.

But if you are at peace with that One, then you can care little what men may do. You can say with the apostles. 'We must obey God rather than men'; you can say with Luther: 'Here I stand, I cannot do otherwise,

God help me. Amen'; you can say with Elisha, 'They that be with us are more than they that be with them'; you can say with Paul: 'It is God that justifieth, who is he that condemneth?' Without that peace of God in your hearts, you will strike little terror into the enemies of the gospel of Christ. You may amass mighty resources for the conflict; you may be great masters of ecclesiastical strategy; you may be very clever, and very zealous too; but I fear that it will be of little avail. There may be a tremendous din; but when the din is over, the Lord's enemies will be in possession of the field. No, there is no other way to be a really good fighter. You cannot fight God's battle against God's enemies unless you are at peace with Him.

But how shall you be at peace with Him? Many ways have been tried. How pathetic is the age-long effort of sinful man to become right with God: sacrifice, lacerations, almsgiving, morality, penance, confession! But alas, it is all of no avail. Still there is that same awful gulf. It may be temporarily concealed: spiritual exercises may conceal it for a time: penance or the confession of sin unto men may give a temporary and apparent relief. But the real trouble remains; the burden is still on the back; Mount Sinai is still ready to shoot forth flames; the soul is still not at peace with God. How then shall peace be obtained?

My friends, it cannot be attained by anything in us. Oh, that that truth could be written in the hearts of every one of you! Oh, that it could be written in letters of flame for all the world to read! Peace with God cannot be attained by any act or any mere experience of man; it cannot be attained by good works, neither can it be attained by confession of sin, neither can it be attained by any psychological results of an act of faith. We can never be at peace with God unless God first be at peace with us. But how can God be at peace with us? Can He be at peace with us by ignoring the guilt of sin, by descending from His throne, by throwing the universe

135

into chaos, by making wrong to be the same as right, by making a dead letter of His holy law, 'The soul that sinneth it shall die,' by treating His eternal laws as though they were the changeable laws of man? Oh, what an abyss were the universe if that were done, what a mad anarchy, what a wild demon-riot! Where could there be peace if God were thus at war with Himself; where could there be a foundation if God's laws were not sure? Oh, no, my friends, peace cannot be attained for man by the great modern method of dragging God down to man's level; peace cannot be attained by denying that right is right and wrong is wrong; peace can nowhere be attained if the awful justice of God stand not forever sure.

How then can we sinners stand before that throne? How can there be peace for us in the presence of the justice of God? How can He be just and yet justify the ungodly? There is one answer to these questions. It is not our answer. Our wisdom could never have discovered it. It is God's answer. It is found in the story of the cross. We deserved eternal death because of sin; the eternal Son of God, because He loved us, and because He was sent by the Father who loved us too, died in our stead, for our sins, upon the cross. That message is despised today; upon it the visible church as well as the world pours out the vials of its scorn, or else does it even less honour by paying it lip-service and then passing it by. Men dismiss it as a 'theory of the atonement,' and fall back upon the customary common-places about a principle of self-sacrifice, or the culmination of a universal law, or a revelation of the love of God, or the hallowing of suffering, or the similarity between Christ's death and the death of soldiers who perished in the great war. In the presence of such blindness, our words often seem vain. We may tell men something of what we think about the cross of Christ, but it is harder to tell them what we feel. We pour forth our tears of gratitude and love; we open to the multitude the depths of our souls; we celebrate a mystery so tender, so holy, that we might think it would soften even a heart of stone. But all to no purpose. The cross remains foolishness to the world, men turn coldly away, and our preaching seems but vain. And then comes the wonder of wonders! The hour comes for some poor soul, even through the simplest and poorest preaching; the message is honoured, not the messenger; there comes a flash of light into the soul, and all is as clear as day. 'He loved me and gave himself for me,' says the sinner at last, as he contemplates the Saviour upon the cross. The burden of sin falls from the back, and a soul enters into the peace of God.

Have you yourselves that peace, my friends? If you have, you will not be deceived by the propaganda of any disloyal church. If you have the peace of God in your hearts, you will never shrink from controversy; you will never be afraid to contend earnestly for the faith. Talk of peace in the present deadly peril of the church, and you show, unless you be strangely ignorant of the conditions that exist, that you have little inkling of the true peace of God. Those who have been at the foot of the cross will not be afraid to go forth under the banner of the cross to a holy war of love.

I know that it is hard to live on the heights of Christian experience. We have had flashes of the true meaning of the cross of Christ; but then come long dull days. What shall we do in those dull times? Shall we cease to witness for Christ; shall we make common cause, in those dull days, with those who would destroy the corporate witness of the church? Perhaps we may be tempted to do so. When there are such enemies in our own souls, we may be tempted to say, What time have we for the opponents without? Such reasoning is plausible. But all the same it is false. We are not saved by keeping ourselves constantly in the proper frame of mind, but we were saved by Christ once for all when we were born again by God's Spirit and were enabled by

Him to put our trust in the Saviour. And the gospel message does not cease to be true because we for the moment have lost sight of the full glory of it. Sad will it be for those to whom we minister if we let our changing moods be determinative of the message that at any moment we proclaim, or if we let our changing moods determine the question whether we shall or shall not stand against the rampant forces of unbelief in the church. We ought to look, not within, but without, for the content of what we are to preach, and for the determination of our witness-bearing; not to our changing feelings and experiences, but to the Bible as the Word of God. Then, and then only, shall we preach, not ourselves, but Christ Jesus the Lord.

Where are you going to stand in the great battle which now rages in the church? Are you going to curry favour with the world by standing aloof; are you going to be 'conservative liberals' or 'liberal conservatives' or 'Christians who do not believe in controversy,' or anything else so self-contradictory and absurd? Are you going to be Christians, but not Christians overmuch? Are you going to stand coldly aloof when God's people fight against ecclesiastical tyranny at home and abroad? Are you going to excuse yourselves by pointing out personal defects in those who contend for the faith today? Are you going to be disloyal to Christ in external testimony until you can make all well within your own soul? Be assured, you will never accomplish your purpose if you adopt such a programme as that. Witness bravely to the truth that you already understand, and more will be given you; but make common cause with those who deny or ignore the gospel of Christ, and the enemy will forever run riot in your life.

There are many hopes that I cherish for you men, with whom I am united by such ties of affection. I hope that you may be gifted preachers; I hope that you may have happy lives; I hope that you may have adequate support for yourselves and for your families; I hope that you may have good churches. But I hope something for you far more than all that. I hope above all that, wherever you are and however your preaching may be received, you may be true witnesses for the Lord Jesus Christ; I hope that there may never be any doubt where *you* stand, but that always you may stand squarely for Jesus Christ, as He is offered to us, not in the experiences of men, but in the blessed written Word of God.

I do not mean that the great issue of the day must be polemically presented in every sermon that you preach. No doubt that would be exceedingly unwise. You should always endeavour to build the people up by simple and positive instruction in the Word. But never will such simple and positive instruction in the Word have the full blessing of God, if, when the occasion does arise to take a stand, you shrink back. God hardly honours the ministry of those who in the hour of decision are ashamed of the gospel of Christ.

But we are persuaded better things of you, my brethren. You have, indeed, your struggles; faith contends against doubt and doubt contends against faith for the possession of your souls. Many of you are called upon to pass through deep waters and to face fiery trials. Never is it an easy process to substitute for the unthinking faith of childhood the fire-tested convictions of full-grown men. But may God bring you through! May God bring you out from the mists of doubt and hesitation into the clear shining of the light of faith! You may not indeed at once attain full clearness; gloomy doubts may arise like angels of Satan to buffet you. But God grant that you may have sufficient clearness to stand at least for Jesus Christ. It will not be easy. Many have been swept from their moorings by the current of the age; a church grown worldly often tyrannises over those who look for guidance to God's Word alone. But this is not the first discouraging time in the history of the church; other times were just as dark, and yet always God has watched over His people, and the darkest hour has sometimes preceded the dawn. So even now God has not left Himself without a witness. In many lands there are those who have faced the great issue of the day and have decided it aright, who have preserved true independence of mind in the presence of the world; in many lands there are groups of Christian people who in the face of ecclesiastical tyranny have not been afraid to stand for Jesus Christ. God grant that you may give comfort to them as you go forth from this seminary; God grant that you may rejoice their hearts by giving them your hand and your voice! To do so you will need courage. Far easier is it to curry favour with the world by abusing those whom the world abuses, by speaking against controversy, by taking a balcony view of the struggle in which God's servants are engaged. But God save you from such a neutrality as that! It has a certain worldly appearance of urbanity and charity. But how cruel it is to burdened souls; how heartless it is to those little ones who are looking to the church for some clear message from God! God save you from being so heartless and so unloving and so cold; God grant, instead, that in all humility, but also in all boldness, in reliance upon God, you may fight the good fight of faith! Peace is indeed yours, the peace of God which passeth all understanding. But that peace is given you, not that you may be onlookers or neutrals in love's battle, but that you may be good soldiers of Jesus Christ.

# 15: *Constraining Love*

*'For the love of Christ constraineth us; because we thus judge, that if one died for all, then were all dead: and that he died for all, that they which live should not henceforth live unto themselves, but unto him which died for them, and rose again'* (2 Cor. 5:14f.).

IN these great verses Paul speaks of love as a constraining force. Love, he says, hems us in. There are certain things which love prevents us from doing.

Earlier in the passage he has spoken of another restraining force – namely, fear. 'Knowing therefore the terror of the Lord,' he says, 'we persuade men.' Since we must all appear before the judgment seat of Christ, it behoves us to stand in fear of Him; and there are many things which, because we shall stand before His judgment seat, we are afraid to do.

That motive of fear is used in many places in the Bible. It is used in the Old Testament. It is used in the New Testament. It is used with particular insistence in the teaching of Jesus. I think it is one of the strangest of modern aberrations when men say it is a degrading and sub-Christian thing to tell man to stand in fear of God. Many passages in the Bible might be summarised by the words: 'The fear of God constraineth us.'

In our text, however, it is something other than fear that is the thing that is said to constrain us or hem us in. It is love. 'The love of Christ,' Paul says, 'constraineth us.'

What then is here meant by the love of Christ? Our first impulse, perhaps, might be to say that it is our love of Christ, the love which we bear to Christ, the love in our hearts for Christ our Saviour. The comparison with verse 11 might perhaps suggest that view. As there the fear which is in our hearts when we think of our standing before the judgment seat of Christ constrains us from doing things that we might otherwise do, so here the love which is in our hearts when we think of what Christ has done for us might seem to be the second constraining force of which Paul speaks.

Now if that is the right interpretation, the verse tells us something that is certainly true. It is certainly true, and eminently in accordance with Paul's teaching elsewhere, that the love of Christ which we have in our hearts restrains us from doing things which otherwise we might do. We refrain from doing those things not only because we are afraid to do them, but also because we love Christ too much to do them. Ah, how powerful a restraining force in the Christian's life is the love he bears to Christ, his Saviour! That love in the Christian's heart is a restraining force even more powerful than any fear.

As a matter of fact, however, that is not Paul's meaning here. The love of Christ which he here says constrains us is not our love for Christ, but it is Christ's love for us. We are restrained from doing evil things, Paul says, by that unspeakable love which Christ manifested when He died for us on the cross.

Well, then, if it is Christ's love for us which constrains us according to this verse, how does Christ's love for us produce that constraining effect in our lives?

The following words give the answer. 'The love of Christ constraineth us,' Paul says, 'because we thus judge, that if one died for all, then were all dead.' I do not think that the translation 'because we thus judge,' though it appears in both the Authorised and in the Revised Version, is strictly accurate. It ought rather to be 'because we *have* thus judged.' The great conviction that Christ died for all and that therefore all died is not formed again and again in Paul's mind as though it were a new conviction, but it has already been formed. It is one of the basic convictions underlying all Paul's Christian life. 'The love of Christ constraineth us,' Paul says, 'because we formed the conviction long ago that Christ died for all and that therefore all died.' Those who have that conviction, as Paul had, already formed in their minds are restrained ever after from doing certain things which otherwise they might do. Since they are convinced that Christ died for them they cannot thereafter do the things that are displeasing to Him – to Him who by His death for them showed that He loved them with such a wonderful love. Once they are convinced that Christ's death was a death for them, their gratitude to the one who died hems them in, restrains them from evil, more effectively than they could have been restrained by prison bars.

That much, I think, is certain in this passage. We have here a true Scriptural basis for the great hymn of Isaac Watts:

> *When I survey the wondrous cross*
> *On which the Prince of Glory*
> *died,*
> *My richest gain I count but loss,*
> *And pour contempt on all my*
> *pride.*

The overpowering love of Christ for us, manifested when He died for us on the cross, calls forth our all in response. Nothing can be so precious to us that we should not give it up to Him who gave Himself there for us on the tree.

But although that is no doubt taught or implied in the passage, a great deal more is taught. There are great depths of additional meaning in the passage, and we must try to explore those depths just a little further before we sit at the table of the Lord.

'The love of Christ constraineth us,' Paul says, 'because we have thus judged, that one died for all, *therefore all died.*' Those are rather strange words, when you come to think of it – 'One died for all, therefore all died.' How does the second of these two propositions follow from the former? Why should we draw from the fact that one died for all the inference that therefore all died? A very different inference might conceivably be drawn. It might be said with more apparent show of reason: 'One died for all, therefore all did *not* die; one died for all, therefore all lived.' When one man dies for others, the usual purpose of his dying is that those others may not have to die; he dies that those others may live.

Yet here we have it said that one died for all and then all died. Apparently the death of Christ did no good to those for whom He died. Apparently He did not succeed in rescuing them from death. Apparently they had to die after all.

It might look at least as though Paul ought to have recognised the contradiction. It might look as though he ought to have said: 'One died for all, *nevertheless* all died.' But he does not recognise the contradiction at all. He puts the death of Christ not as something that might conceivably prevent the death of others, but as something that actually brought with it the death of others. He says not: 'One died for all, nevertheless all died,' but: 'One died for all, *therefore* all died.'

The thing might seem strange to the unbeliever; it might seem strange to the man who should come to this passage without having read the rest of the Bible and in particular the rest of the Epistles of Paul. But it does not seem at all strange to the Christian; it does not seem at all strange to the man who reads it in connection with the great central teaching of the Word of God regarding the cross of Christ.

Christ died for all, therefore all died – of course, that is so because Christ was the representative of all when He died. The death that He died on the cross was in itself the death of all. Since Christ was the representative of all, therefore all may have been said to have died there on the cross outside the walls of Jerusalem when Christ died.

We may imagine a dialogue between the law of God and a sinful man.

'Man,' says the law of God, 'have you obeyed my commands?'

'No,' says the sinner, 'I have transgressed them in thought, word, and deed.'

'Well, then, sinner,' says the law, 'have you paid the penalty which I have pronounced upon those who have disobeyed? Have you died in the sense that I meant when I said, "The soul that sinneth it shall die"?'

'Yes,' says the sinner, 'I have died. That penalty that you pronounced upon my sin has been paid.'

'What do you mean,' says the law, 'by saying that you have died? You do not look as though you had died. You look as though you were very much alive.'

'Yes,' says the sinner, 'I have died. I died there on the cross outside the walls of Jerusalem; for Jesus died there as my representative and my substitute. I died there so far as the penalty of the law was concerned.'

'You say Christ is your representative and substitute,' says the law. 'Then I have indeed no further claim of penalty against you. The curse which I pronounced against your sin has indeed been fulfilled. My threatenings are very terrible, but I have nothing to say against those for whom Christ died.'

That, my friends, is what Paul means by the tremendous 'therefore,' when he says: 'One died for all, *therefore* all died.' On that 'therefore' hangs all our hope for time and for eternity.

But what does he mean by 'all'? 'One died for *all*,' he says, 'therefore all died.' He seems to lay considerable emphasis upon that word 'all.' What does he mean by it?

Well, I suppose our Christian brethren in other churches, our Christian brethren who are opposed to the Reformed Faith might be tempted to make that word 'all' mean, in this passage, 'all men'; they might be tempted to make it refer to the whole human race. They might be tempted to interpret the words 'Christ died for all men everywhere whether Christians or not.'

But if they are tempted to make it mean that, they ought to resist the temptation, since this passage is really a very dangerous passage for them to lay stress on in support of their view.

In the first place, the context is dead against it. It is rather strongly against the view that 'Christ died for all' means here 'Christ died for all men.' All through this passage Paul is speaking not of the relation of Christ to all men, but of the relation of Christ to the church.

In the second place, the view that 'Christ died for all' means 'Christ died for all men' proves too much. The things that Paul says in this passage about those for whom Christ died do not fit those who merely have the gospel offered to them; they fit only those who accept the gospel for the salvation of their souls. Can it be said of all men, including those who reject the gospel or have never heard it, that they died when Christ died on the cross; can it be said of them that they no longer live unto themselves but unto the Christ who died for them? Surely these things cannot be said of all men, and therefore the word 'all' does not mean all men.

Perhaps, indeed, it will be said that Paul is speaking only of the purpose of Christ in dying for all men, without implying that that purpose was accomplished. Perhaps, it will be said, he means only that Christ died for all men with the purpose that all men might live to Him who died for them, without at all implying how many of those for whom Christ died actually accomplished that purpose by living in that way.

Well – quite aside from the difficulty of supposing that God's purposes ever fail – I can only say that if that meaning be attributed to the passage the force of the passage is, to say the least, seriously impaired. Did Christ upon the cross die merely to make possible my salvation? Did He die merely for the great mass of humanity and then leave it to the decision of individuals in that mass whether they would make any use of what Christ purchased for them at such cost? Was I, in the thought of the Son of God when He died there on Calvary, merely one in the great mass of persons who might possibly at some future time accept the benefits of His death?

I tell you, my friends, if I thought that – if, in other words, I became a consistent Arminian instead of a Calvinist – I should feel almost as though the light had forever gone out of my soul. No, indeed, my friends, Christ did not die there on Calvary merely to make possible our salvation. He died to save us. He died not merely to provide a general benefit for the human race from which we might at some future time draw, as from some general fund, what is needed for the salvation of our souls. No, thank God, He died there on the cross for us individually. He called us, when He died for us, by our names. He loved us not as infinitesimal particles in the mass of the human race, but He loved us every one.

Do you ask how that could be? Do you ask how Christ when He died could have in His mind and heart every one of the millions of those who had been saved under the old dispensation and who were to be saved in the long centuries that were to come? I will tell you how it could be. It could be because Christ is God. Being God He knows us every one, with an intimacy that is far greater than the intimacy of the tenderest mother's love.

People say that Calvinism is a dour, hard creed. How broad and comforting, they say, is the doctrine of a universal atonement, the doctrine that Christ died equally for all men there upon the cross! How narrow and harsh, they say, is this Calvinistic doctrine – one of the 'five points' of Calvinism – this doctrine of the 'limited atonement,' this doctrine that Christ died for the elect of God in a sense in which He did not die for the unsaved!

But do you know, my friends, it is surprising that men say that. It is surprising that they regard the doctrine of a universal atonement as being a comforting doctrine. In reality it is a very gloomy doctrine indeed. Ah, if it were only a doctrine of a universal salvation, instead of a doctrine of a universal atonement, then it would no doubt be a very comforting doctrine; then no doubt it would conform wonderfully well to what we in our puny wisdom might have thought the course of the world should have been. But a universal atonement without a universal salvation is a cold, gloomy doctrine indeed. To say that Christ died for all men alike and that then not all men are saved, to say that Christ died for humanity simply in the mass, and that the choice of those who out of that mass are saved depends upon the greater receptivity of some as compared with others – that is a doctrine that takes from the gospel much of its sweetness and much of its joy. From the cold universalism of that Arminian creed we turn ever again with a new thankfulness to the warm and tender individualism of our Reformed Faith, which we believe to be in accord with God's holy Word. Thank God we can say every one, as we contemplate Christ upon the cross, not just: 'He died for the mass of humanity, and how glad I am that I am amid that mass,' but: 'He loved me and gave Himself for me; my name was written from all eternity upon His heart, and when He hung and suffered there on the cross He thought of men, even me, as one for whom in His grace He was willing to die.'

That is what Paul means when he says, 'One died for all, therefore all died.' But is that all that Paul says? No, he says something more; and we must consider briefly that something more, before we turn away from this marvellous passage.

'All of us died,' Paul says, 'since it was as our

representative that Christ died.' But what then? What becomes afterwards of those who have thus died to the curse of the law? Are they free thereafter to live as they please, because the penalty of their sins has been paid?

Paul gives the answer in no uncertain terms. 'One died for all,' he says, 'therefore all died, that they which live should not henceforth live unto themselves but unto him which died for them, and rose again.'

Some people upon this earth, he says, have passed through a wonderful thing! They have died. That is, Christ died for them as their representative. They have died so far as concerns the death which the law of God pronounces as the penalty of sin. They died there on Calvary in the Person of Christ their Saviour. But what of them now? Look at them, and you might think if you were a very superficial observer that they are living very much as before. They are subject to all the petty limitations of human life. They are walking the streets of Corinth or of Philadelphia. They are going about their daily tasks. They might seem to be very much the same. Ah, but, says Paul, they are not really the same; a great change has taken place in them. They are living upon this earth. Yes, that is granted. They are living in the flesh. Very true. But their lives – their humdrum, working lives upon this earth – have now an entirely new direction. Formerly they were living unto themselves; now they are living unto Christ. What greater change could there possibly be than that?

Christ had that change definitely in view, Paul says, when He died for them on the cross. He did not die for them on the cross in order that they might live with impunity in sin. He did not die for them on the cross in order that they might continue to live for themselves. He died that they might live for Him.

'One died for all, therefore all died; and he died for all that they which live should not henceforth live unto themselves' – let us stop just there for a moment to notice that at that point the grand circle is complete.

149

Paul has got back to the assertion with which he began; only now he has shown gloriously how it is that that assertion is true. He began by saying, 'The love of Christ constraineth us,' and now he has shown how that constraint has been brought about. 'The love of Christ constraineth us; because we have thus judged, that one died for all, therefore all died; and that he died for all, that they which live should not henceforth live for themselves.' 'Should not henceforth live unto themselves' – that is the constraint of which Paul started out to speak. A man who may not live unto himself is indeed under constraint. All the impulses of fallen man lead him to live unto himself. A hundred selfish passions and appetites crave free course. Yet here are fallen men who check the free course of those selfish passions and appetites. What has caused them to do so? The answer is 'Christ's love.' He loved them. Loving them He died for them on the cross. Dying for them on the cross He wiped out the curse of the law against them, that in the new life that they then began by His Spirit to live they might by thinking on His death be led to live no longer unto themselves. What a wonderful restraining force was exerted by Christ's dying love! How many things freely done by the men of the world, the Christian is restrained by Christ's love from doing!

Yes, it is indeed true that if we are real Christians 'the love of Christ constraineth us.' Paul is not afraid to use a very drastic word in this connection. He is not afraid to say: 'The love of Christ hems us in, surrounds us on every side as with a barrier or wall.'

The reason why he is not afraid to say that is that he is going to wipe the paradox out in this very same verse; he is going to show his readers at once that the restraint of which he speaks is the most glorious freedom; he is going to make abundantly plain right in this very passage that the Christian life is not a cabined and confined life at all but a life that is marvellously rich and free. The Christian is restrained from doing certain things. True! But he is restrained from doing those things not in order that he may do nothing at all, but in order that he may do other things that are infinitely more worth while. He is restrained from doing evil things that he may do the things that are good; he is restrained from doing things that bring death in order that he may do things that belong to eternal life.

What are those good things in the doing of which Christian freedom is shown? Ah, how wonderfully does Paul sum them up in this glorious verse! Listen to the grand climax with which the sentence ends. 'The love of Christ constraineth us,' he says, 'because we have thus judged, that one died for all, therefore all died; and that he died for all that they which live should not henceforth live unto themselves, *but unto him which died for them.*' 'But unto him which died for them' – ah, there is the refutation forever of the charge brought by carnal men that the Christian life is a narrow and restricted life, life hemmed in by 'Thou shalt not's' but without high aspirations or a worthy goal. No, it is not a narrow and restricted life at all. What sweet and lovely thing in human living may not be included in that one great business of living unto Christ? Art, you say? Is that excluded? No, indeed! Christ made the beauty of the world, and He made men that they might enjoy that beauty and celebrate it unto His praise. Science? All the wonders of the universe are His. He made all, and the true man of science has the privilege of looking just a little way into His glorious works. Every high and worthy human pursuit may be ennobled and enlarged by being consecrated unto Christ. But highest of all is the privilege of bringing other souls to Him. That privilege belongs not only to the wise and learned. It belongs to the humblest Christians. To be the instrument in saving a soul from death – what more wonderful adventure can there be than that? No, the Christian life is not a narrow and restricted life. It is a life most wonderfully free. What rich harvest fields it offers, what broad prospects, what glittering mountain-heights!

In all that life of high endeavour the Christian thinks always of the One to whom he owes it all, the One who died. Ever does he remember that one died for all and that therefore all died. What depth of love in the Christian's heart is called forth by that story of the dying love of Christ! What a barrier it is against selfishness and sin, what an incentive to brave and loving deeds! He died for all, and in the true Christian's life the purpose of His dying is indeed fulfilled that they which live should not henceforth live unto themselves but unto Him which died for them.

We have almost finished. We have read the passage almost to the end. But there is one word that we have so far not touched. It is the very last word. Sadly incomplete would our exposition be if we did not now notice that tremendous word.

'The love of Christ constraineth us; because we have thus judged, that one died for all, therefore all died; and that he died for all, that they which live should not henceforth live unto themselves, but unto him which died for them, and *rose again*.'

'And *rose again*' – that is the word (one word it is in the Greek) that we must notice at last before we sit down together at the table of our Lord.

How does our thought of the death of Christ restrain us from evil and inspire us to good? Is it merely like the thought of some dear one who has gone? Is it merely the thought of that last smile on a mother's face; is it merely like our thought of the last touch of her vanished hand; is it merely like the memory of those last loving words when she bade us to be true and good?

Well, we do think of the death of our Lord in some way as that. We commemorate that death today in the broken bread and the poured out cup. We think of that simple story in the Gospels which tells how He broke the bread with His disciples, endured mocking of wicked men, was taken outside the walls, and died for the love that He bore to us sinners. And as we think on that story our hearts melt within us and we are ashamed to offend against such love. We say to ourselves, in the words of the sweet Christian hymn:

> *O, dearly, dearly has He loved!*
> *And we must love Him too,*
> *And trust in His redeeming blood,*
> *And try His works to do.*

But is that all? No, it is not all, my friends. It is not all, because that One who there died for us is now alive. He is not dead but is with us in blessed presence today. He died for all that they which live should not live unto themselves, but unto Him which died for them and *rose again*. We do more than commemorate His death when we sit around the table this morning. We rejoice also in His presence. And as we go forth from this place we must live as those who are ever in His sight. Are we in temptation? Let us remember that He who died for us, and who by His dying love constrains us that we fall not into sin, is with us today, and is grieved if we dishonour Him in our lives. It is not to a memory merely that we Christians have dedicated ourselves. It is to the service of a living Saviour. Let us remember always that 'He died for all, that they which live should not henceforth live unto themselves but unto him which died for them and *rose again*.'

This morning we, a little branch of his church universal, are gathered for the first time together around His table. We shall go forth from this service into the deliberations of this Assembly and then into the varied work of the church.

If we remember what this service commemorates, there are certain things which we shall be constrained by Christ's love not to do.

We shall be constrained, for example, not to weaken in the stand which we have taken for the sake of Christ. How many movements have begun bravely like this one, and then have been deceived by Satan – have been deceived by Satan into belittling controversy, condoning sin and error, seeking favour from the world or from a worldly church, substituting a worldly urbanity for Christian love. May Christ's love indeed constrain us that we may not thus fall!

We shall be constrained, in the second place, from seeking unworthily our own advantage or preferment, and from being jealous of the advantage or preferment of our brethren. May Christ's love indeed constrain us that we fall not into faults such as these!

We shall be constrained, in the third place, from stifling discussion for the sake of peace and from (as has been said) 'shelving important issues in moments of silent prayer.' May Christ's love constrain us from such a misuse of the sacred and blessed privilege of prayer! May Christ's love prevent us from doing anything to hinder our brethren from giving legitimate expression to the convictions of their minds and hearts!

We shall be constrained, in short, from succumbing to the many dangers which always beset a movement such as this. Christ's love alone will save us from such dangers.

But Christ's love will do more than restrain us from evil. It will lead us also into good. It will do more than prevent us from living unto ourselves. It will also lead us to live unto Him.

What a wonderful open door God has placed before the church of today. A pagan world, weary and sick, often distrusting its own modern gods. A saving gospel strangely entrusted to us unworthy messengers. A divine Book with unused resources of glory and power. Ah, what a marvellous opportunity, my brethren! What a privilege to proclaim not some partial system of truth but the full, glorious system which God has revealed in His Word, and which is summarised in the wonderful Standards of our Faith! What a privilege to get those hallowed instruments, in which that truth is summarised, down from the shelf and write them in patient instruction, by the blessing of the Holy Spirit, upon the tablets of the children's hearts! What a privilege to present our historic Standards in all their fulness in the pulpit and at the teacher's desk and in the Christian home! What a privilege to do that for the one reason that those Standards present, not a 'man-made creed,' but what God has told us in His holy Word! What a privilege to proclaim that same system of divine truth to the unsaved! What a privilege to carry the message of the cross, unshackled by compromising associations, to all the world! What a privilege to send it to foreign lands! What a privilege to proclaim it to the souls of people who sit in nominally Christian churches and starve for lack of the bread of life! Oh, yes, what a privilege and what a joy, my brethren! Shall we lose that joy for any selfishness or jealousy; shall we lose it for any of the sins into which every one of us without exception is prone to fall?

Only one thing can prevent us from losing it, my brethren. Only one thing can bestow it upon us in all its fulness. That one thing is the love of Jesus Christ our Saviour – the love that we celebrate as we sit this morning around the table of our Lord. That love alone can restrain us from the sins that will if unchecked destroy this church's life – the sins of the preacher of this morning, the sins of those to whom he preaches. That alone can send us forth rejoicing to live for Him who died. As we sit now at His table, and commemorate His dying love, may the blessed words that we have read together this morning sink deep into our minds and hearts and bear fruit in our lives. May it now indeed be true of us that: 'The love of Christ constraineth us; because we thus judge, that if one died for all, then were all dead: and that he died for all, that they which live should not henceforth live unto themselves, but unto him which died for them, and rose again.'

cannot set forth clearly what a thing is without placing it in contrast with what it is not. All definition proceeds by way of exclusion. How utterly shallow, then, is the notion that the church ought to make its teaching positive and not negative – the notion that controversy should be avoided and truth should be maintained without attack upon error! The simple fact is that truth cannot possibly be maintained in any such way. Truth can be maintained only when it is sharply differentiated from error. It is no wonder, then, that the great creeds of the church, as also the great revivals of religion in the church, were born in theological controversy. The increasing richness and the increasing precision of Christian doctrine were brought about very largely by the necessity of excluding one alien element after another from the teaching of the church.

In recent years the church has often entered upon an exactly opposite course of procedure. It has constructed what purport to be doctrinal statements, but these supposed doctrinal statements are constructed for a purpose which is just the opposite of the purpose that governed the formation of the great historic creeds.

The historic creeds were exclusive of error; they were intended to exclude error; they were intended to set forth the Biblical teaching in sharp contrast with what was opposed to the Biblical teaching, in order that the purity of the church might be preserved. These modern statements, on the contrary, are inclusive of error. They are designed to make room in the church for just as many people and for just as many types of thought as possible.

There are entirely too many denominations in this country, says the modern ecclesiastical efficiency expert. Obviously, many of them must be merged. But the trouble is, they have different creeds. Here is one church, for example, that has a clearly Calvinistic creed; here is another whose creed is just as clearly Arminian, let us say, and anti-Calvinistic. How in the

# 16: *The Creeds and Doctrinal Advance*

LAST Sunday afternoon, in the first of our talks of this winter, I spoke to you in a summary sort of way about the progress of Christian doctrine in the church. I showed how the church advanced from the very meagre statement which is commonly called the Apostles' Creed, on through the great early ecumenical creeds, setting forth the doctrines of the Trinity and the Person of Christ, and through Augustine, with his presentation of the doctrine of sin and divine grace, to the Reformation and to Calvin. I showed how that type of doctrine which follows on the path in which Calvin moved is called the Reformed Faith.

The Reformed Faith has found expression in a number of great creeds which all exhibit the same general type. One of these creeds is the Heidelberg Catechism. That is the official doctrinal standard of certain American churches whose members came originally from the continent of Europe. These churches are called 'Reformed' churches. Another of the great creeds setting forth the Reformed Faith is the one that consists of the Westminster Confession of Faith and the Larger and Shorter Catechisms. They are the official doctrinal standards of certain American churches whose members originally came chiefly from Scotland and Ireland. These are called 'Presbyterian' churches. It is these doctrinal standards to which I have frequently referred in these little talks that I have been giving on Sunday afternoons during the past two winters.

Perhaps one question was in the minds of some of you as I reviewed the progress of Christian doctrine last Sunday afternoon. Why should the progress be thought to have been brought to a close in the seventeenth century, when the Westminster Confession of Faith and Catechisms were produced? Why should there not be still further doctrinal advance? If the church advanced in doctrine up to the time of the Westminster Standards, why should it now not proceed still further on its onward march?

Well, there is no essential reason why it should not do so. However before it attempts to do so, it is very important for it to understand precisely what Christian doctrine is. It should understand very clearly that Christian doctrine is just a setting forth of what the Bible teaches. At the foundation of Christian doctrine is the acceptance of the full truthfulness of the Bible as the Word of God.

That is often forgotten by those who today undertake to write confessional statements. Let us give expression to our Christian experience, they say, in forms better suited to the times in which we are living than are the older creeds of the church. So they sit down and concoct various forms of words, which they represent as being on a plane with the great creeds of Christendom.

When they do that, they are simply forgetting what the creeds of Christendom are. The creeds of Christendom are not expressions of Christian experience. They are summary statements of what God has told us in His Word. Far from the subject-matter of the creeds being derived from Christian experience, it is Christian experience which is based upon the truth contained in the creeds; and the truth contained in the creeds is derived from the Bible, which is the Word of God. Groups of people that undertake to write a creed without believing in the full truthfulness of the Bible, and without taking the subject-matter of their creed from that inspired Word of God, are not at all taking an additional step on the pathway on which the great Christian creeds moved; rather, they are moving in an exactly opposite direction. What they are doing has

nothing whatever to do with that grand progress Christian doctrine of which I spoke last Sunday. F from continuing the advance of Christian doctrine th are starting something entirely different, and th something different, we may add, is doomed to failu from the start.

The first prerequisite, then, for any advance Christian doctrine is that those who would engage ir should believe in the full truthfulness of the Bible a should endeavour to make their doctrine simply presentation of what the Bible teaches.

There are other principles also that must be obser if there is to be real doctrinal advance. For one thi all real doctrinal advance proceeds in the directio1 greater precision and fulness of doctrinal statem Just run over in your minds again the history of great creeds of the church. How meagre was the called Apostles' Creed, first formulated in the sec century! How far more precise and full were the cr of the great early councils, beginning with the Ni creed in A.D. 325! How much more precise and vastly richer still were the Reformation creeds especially our Westminster Confession of Faith!

This increasing precision and this increasing ness of doctrinal statement were arrived at particu by way of refutation of errors as they successively a At first the church's convictions about some poin doctrine were implicit rather than explicit. They not carefully defined. They were assumed rather expressly stated. Then some new teaching arose church reflected on the matter, comparing the teaching with the Bible. It found the new teachi be contrary to the Bible. As over against the teaching, it set forth precisely what the true Bi teaching on the point is. So a great doctrine was c stated in some great Christian creed.

That method of doctrinal advance is, of cour accord with the fundamental laws of the mind

world are we going to get the two together? Why, obviously, says the ecclesiastical efficiency expert, the thing to do is to tone down that Calvinistic creed; just smooth off its sharp angles, until Arminians will be able to accept it. Or else we can do something better still. We can write an entirely new creed that will contain only what Arminianism and Calvinism have in common, so that it can serve as the basis for some proposed new 'United Church.'

Such are the methods of modern church-unionism. Those methods are carried even to much greater lengths today than in the hypothetical example that I have just mentioned. Calvinism and Arminianism, which I have mentioned in this example, though they differ very widely, are both of them types of evangelical Christian belief. But many of these modern statements are so worded as to gain the assent not only of men who hold different varieties of Christian belief, like Calvinism and Arminianism, but also of men who hold to no really Christian belief at all.

Take some of the great world-conferences on missions, for example. At those conferences are represented men who believe in the virgin birth of Christ, His substitutionary atonement, His bodily resurrection and other essential elements of the historic Christian faith, and also there are represented men who oppose these things or belittle them as entirely unimportant. There are many speeches – some of them from men generally thought to be evangelical Christians, some of them from distinguished Modernists. After days of such speech-making, a common statement of belief is presented and is unanimously adopted.

What is that common statement like? Well, its outstanding characteristic is apt to be just what would be expected from the circumstances under which it was adopted. Its outstanding characteristic is apt to be a complete absence of character – a complete and unrelieved vagueness. Really, when I read some of these

161

statements, I am amazed at the amount of printer's ink which it is possible to use up without saying anything at all. Words and phrases are indeed used which formerly had a meaning, and which ought to have a meaning now; but these words have been explained away so long that in themselves they now afford no evidence whatever as to what the person who uses them really believes.

When such a vague statement is issued there are always found people who rejoice. Was it not great cause for rejoicing, they say, that our differences were all ironed out? We had been afraid, they say, lest some one would have objected to an evangelical statement like the statement of that missionary council; but our fears were groundless, and even those at the council who were accounted most radical consented to the statement like all the rest. Was not that perfectly splendid?

No, I say when people talk to me in that fashion, I do not think it was splendid at all. I think it was very sad. I should not have thought it to be splendid even if the statement of the council had been really evangelical instead of only apparently so. Is it splendid when men who are plainly out of accord with an evangelical statement acquiesce in the issuance of it and then go on exactly as before in their opposition to the things that the statement contains? I am bound to think that that is the reverse of splendid. But, as a matter of fact, the statement in most cases is not really evangelical at all, but utterly vague. It is so worded as to offend no one. At least, it is so worded as to offend no one except those old-fashioned souls who are hungry for the bread of life and are not satisfied with a type of Christian doctrine that is afraid of its own shadow. The statement is usually so worded that the Modernists can interpret its traditional phrases in their own fashion; and, on the other hand, it is so worded that persons who are evangelical, or think they are evangelical, can bring it back to their constituency as a great diplomatic triumph of orthodoxy. Its great object is to avoid offence. The consequence is that it is just about as far removed as possible from the gospel of Christ. For the gospel of Christ is always offensive in the extreme.

When we pass from these modern statements to the great creeds, what a difference we discover! Instead of wordiness we find conciseness; instead of an unwillingness to offend, clear delimitation of truth from error; instead of obscurity, clearness; instead of vagueness, the utmost definiteness and precision.

All these differences are rooted in a fundamental difference of purpose. These modern statements are intended to show how little of truth we can get along with and still be Christians, whereas the great creeds of the church are intended to show how much of truth God has revealed to us in His Word. Let us sink our differences, say the authors of these modern statements, and get back to a few bare essentials; let us open our Bibles, say the authors of the great Christian creeds, and seek to unfold the full richness of truth that the Bible contains. Let us be careful, say the authors of these modern statements, not to discourage any of the various tendencies of thought that find a lodgment in the church; let us give all diligence, say the authors of the great Christian creeds, to exclude deadly error from the official teaching of the church, in order that thus the church may be a faithful steward of the mysteries of God.

The difference of purpose is a fundamental difference indeed. But I am inclined to think that there is another difference that is more fundamental still. The most important difference of all is that the authors of these modern statements do not really believe firmly in the existence of truth at all. Since doctrine, they say, is merely the expression of Christian experience, doctrines change and yet the fundamental experience remains the same. One generation expresses its Christian experience in one doctrine, and then another generation may express the same Christian experience in an exactly opposite doctrine. So the Modernism of today becomes the orthodoxy of tomorrow, which in turn gives place to a new Modernism, and so on in an infinite series. No doctrine, according to that theory, can remain valid forever; doctrine must change as the forms of thought change from age to age.

When you ask a person of this way of thinking whether he accepts the great historic creeds of the church, he says to you: 'Oh yes, certainly I do. I accept them as expressions of the faith of the church. The Apostles' Creed expressed admirably the faith of the ancient church; the Westminster Confession was an admirable expression of the faith of men of the seventeenth century. But as for making these creeds the expression of my faith, of course I cannot possibly do that. I must express my faith in the terms that are suited to the people of the twentieth century. So I must construct a new and entirely different statement to be the creed of modern men.'

'Well, then,' I ask such a man, 'do you think your statement is more true than those historic creeds?'

'Not at all,' says he, if he really works out the logical conclusions of his conception of creeds; 'those creeds were true expressions of Christian experience, mine also is a true expression of essentially the same experience in the forms of thought that are suited to the present age, but my statement is not a bit more true than those ancient creeds; it, not a bit more than they, can lay claim to permanency; it is true in the present age, but that does not mean at all that it will remain true in the generations to come.'

What shall we say about this sceptical notion of what truth is – this sceptical notion with regard to the nature of Christian doctrine? Well, we can say at least this about it: that it is entirely different from the notion that was cherished by those who gave us the great creeds of the church. Those who gave us the great creeds of the church, unlike the authors of these modern statements, believed that the creeds that they produced were true – true in the plain man's sense of the word 'truth'. They believed that the truth they contained would remain true forever.

It is time now to get back to the question with which this talk began. Is it or is it not possible that there should be still further advance in Christian doctrine?

Yes, we answer, but only provided the necessary conditions for any real doctrinal advance be observed.

If there is to be any doctrinal advance, we must believe that doctrine is the setting forth of what is true, not a mere expression of religious experience in symbolic form; we must believe, in the second place, that doctrine is the setting forth of that particular truth that is contained in the Bible, which we must hold to be truly God's Word and altogether free from the errors found in other books; we must endeavour, in the third place, not to make doctrine as meagre and vague as possible in order that it shall make room for error, but as full and precise as possible in order that it shall exclude error and set forth the wonderful richness of what God has revealed. Ignore these conditions, and you have doctrinal retrogression or decadence; only if you observe them can you possibly have doctrinal advance.

Such doctrinal advance is certainly conceivable. It is perfectly conceivable that the church should examine the particular errors of the present day and should set forth over against them, even more clearly than is done in the existing creeds, the truth that is contained in God's Word. But I am bound to say that I think such doctrinal advance to be just now extremely unlikely. We are living in a time of widespread intellectual as well as moral decadence, and the visible church has unfortunately not kept free from this decadence. Christian education has been sadly neglected; learning has been despised; and real meditation has become almost a lost art. For these reasons, and other still more important reasons, I think it is clear that ours is not a creed-making age. Intellectual and moral indolence like ours do not constitute the soil out of which great Christian creeds may be expected to grow.

But even if ours were a creed-making age, I doubt very much that the doctrinal advance which it or any future age might produce would be comparable to the advance which found expression in the great historic creeds. I think it may well turn out that Christian doctrine in its great outlines, as set forth, for example, in the Westminster Confession of Faith, is now essentially complete. There may be improvements in statement here and there, in the interests of greater precision, but hardly any such great advance as that which was made, for example, at the time of Augustine or at the Reformation. All the great central parts of the Biblical system of doctrine have already been studied by the church and set forth in great creeds.

We need not be too much surprised to discover that that is the case. The subject matter of Christian doctrine, it must be remembered, is fixed. It is found in the Scriptures of the Old and New Testaments, to which nothing can be added.

Let no one say that the recognition of that fact brings with it a static condition of the human mind or is inimical to progress. On the contrary, it removes the shackles from the human mind and opens up untold avenues of progress.

The truth is, there can be no real progress unless there is something that is fixed. Archimedes said, 'Give me a place to stand, and I will move the world.' Well, Christian doctrine provides that place to stand. Unless there be such a place to stand, all progress is an illusion. The very idea of progress implies something fixed. There is no progress in a kaleidoscope.

That is the trouble with the boasted progress of our modern age. The Bible at the start was given up.

Nothing was to be regarded as fixed. All truth was regarded as relative. What has been the result? I will tell you. An unparalleled decadence – liberty prostrate, slavery stalking almost unchecked through the earth, the achievements of centuries crumbling in the dust, sweetness and decency despised, all meaning regarded as having been taken away from human life. What is the remedy? I will tell you that too. A return to God's Word! We had science for the sake of science, and got the World War; we had art for art's sake, and got ugliness gone mad; we had man for the sake of man and got a world of robots – men made into machines. Is it not time for us to come to ourselves, like the prodigal in a far country? Is it not time for us to seek real progress by a return to the living God?

# 17: *Christ Our Redeemer*

LAST Sunday afternoon we began to speak of the second of the three offices which Christ executes as our Redeemer. The three offices are the offices of a prophet, of a priest, and of a king. Last Sunday afternoon we began to speak about Christ's office of a priest.

It became evident at the start that in dealing with Christ's office of a priest we are dealing with the heart of the gospel, because we are dealing with the cross of Christ. By His death, the Bible teaches, Christ made the one and all-sufficient sacrifice for sin. That is the great doctrine of the atonement. Nothing, from the point of view of the Bible, can possibly be more important for mankind than that.

Well, then, in thus exalting the priestly work of Christ, are we depreciating His prophetic work, with which we have been dealing in a number of the preceding talks in this series? That is very far from being the case, and before I go further I want to show you why it is far from being the case; I want to say a few words just upon the relation between Christ's work as a priest, with which we are now going to deal, and Christ's work as a prophet, with which we have hitherto dealt.

I think I can present the relationship in the fewest possible words by just saying that in Christ's priestly work He died for us, and then in His prophetic work He tells us the story of how He died for us. In His priestly work He did the thing that forms the substance of the gospel, and then in His prophetic work He proclaims the gospel Himself to us. In His priestly work He did the thing that made it possible that there should be a gospel to preach, and then in His prophetic work He actually preaches the gospel to us in order that, through the receiving of the gospel, our souls may be saved.

How foolish, then, it is to say either that Christ's work as a priest or that His work as a prophet could possibly stand alone! No, they stand together. Without His work as a priest there would have been no gospel to preach, and without His work as a prophet there would have been no preaching of the gospel. Thank God, Christ has done both! He died on the cross that there might be a gospel to preach, and then very sweetly has He brought the gospel Himself to those for whom He died.

Ignoring these simple facts, so plain in the Bible, modern unbelievers are in the habit of telling us that we ought not to be very much interested in the gospel *about* Jesus but ought instead to devote our attention to the gospel *of* Jesus. We need not be interested, they say, in the exact meaning of what Christ did when He died on the cross; we need not be much interested in the question of what is meant when we say we believe in the 'deity' of Christ; we need not be much interested in the question of whether His body really came out of the tomb on the first Easter morning; we need not be much interested in the question of whether He will really in any literal sense come again.

People used to be interested in these questions, we are told. They used to set up theories of the atonement; they used to maintain, in particular, that on the cross Jesus died as a sacrifice to satisfy divine justice and reconcile us to God. They used to set up theories regarding the Person of Christ; they used to maintain that Christ is God and man in two distinct natures and one person for ever. They used to insist also on one particular view of the resurrection; they used to maintain that on the third day the tomb became empty because the body of the Lord Jesus was raised. They used to insist also on the personal return of Christ; they used to maintain, as though it were very important indeed for our souls, that at the end of the present age we shall see our Saviour face to face.

These things, say the unbelievers about whom I am now speaking, constitute a gospel *about* Jesus. But, they say, we are no longer interested in that gospel *about* Jesus. Instead, we are interested in the gospel *of* Jesus; we are interested in the gospel that He Himself actually preached. We are interested in the way of living in which He walked and in which He called on His followers to walk. We are interested, in other words, not in a gospel that sets Jesus forth, but in the gospel that He set forth, the gospel that He preached when He walked by the shores of the Sea of Galilee.

If, then, you ask the people who talk in this fashion what that gospel of Jesus, which they cherish in place of the gospel about Jesus, actually was, they will usually tell you, with more or less clearness, that it was a simple proclamation of the Fatherhood of God and the brotherhood of man, or a simple proclamation of a kingdom of God that is essentially just the realisation of a high social ideal. Let us stop disputing about the meaning of the cross of Christ, they say; let us stop disputing about any other doctrinal questions; and, instead, let us just get up and obey Jesus' commands. That will honour Jesus more, they say, than all the theories of the atonement that have ever been proposed.

People who talk in this fashion seem to think that they are somehow glorifying Jesus more and are somehow getting closer to Him than was done by the people who used to proclaim the old gospel. Are we not getting closer to Christ, they say to themselves, if we preach His own gospel rather than merely a gospel about Him?

But a little reflection will show that that is far from being the case. I may preach the gospel *of* Spurgeon or the gospel *of* D. L. Moody or the gospel *of* Calvin – that is, I may preach the same gospel as that which they preached. But what blasphemy it would be to say that

I preach a gospel about Spurgeon or a gospel about D. L. Moody or a gospel about Calvin or even a gospel about Paul! If I should do that, I should be putting these preachers into a position which belongs only to Christ. I may preach the gospel that they preach but I certainly do not preach a gospel that has them as its content. I may preach the gospel of Calvin or the gospel of Paul, but I do not preach Calvin and I do not preach Paul. I preach Christ alone, as they preached Christ alone.

It is from this unique place that these modern unbelievers are dethroning Christ when they say that they are not interested in the gospel about Christ and are only interested in the gospel of Christ. They are willing to admit that Jesus was an excellent teacher and example, and that we cannot do better than repeat His teaching and follow His example. But they have not the slightest inkling of the fact that He is the substance of the gospel. They have not the slightest inkling of the fact that the gospel consists in the good news of the way in which He saved us by His precious blood.

Well, then, in thus insisting, against these unbelievers, that the gospel is a gospel about Jesus, in thus insisting that it is a gospel that has Him as its substance, that proclaims Him, do we mean to say that it is not also a gospel that He Himself preached? We mean nothing of the kind. On the contrary we insist that it is the gospel that He Himself preached. Two winters ago, when we were treating the picture of Jesus in the Gospels, we showed how baseless is the contention of modern unbelief that Jesus kept His own person out of His gospel and merely asked people to lead the same kind of religious life as that which He Himself lived. We saw how pervasive was His presentation of His own Person as the divine Saviour and the final Judge of all the earth. We saw how that presentation runs even through the Sermon on the Mount, to which modern unbelievers are wont particularly to appeal. We saw how utterly contrary to all our sources of historical information is this modern notion that Jesus was simply the founder of Christianity because He was the first Christian. We saw how all our sources of historical information represent Jesus as offering Himself to men as the object of their faith.

Do you not see, my friends, what the real state of the case is? It is not correct to say that we Christians proclaim the gospel of Jesus in distinction from a gospel about Jesus. It is equally incorrect to say that we preach a gospel about Jesus in distinction from the gospel of Jesus. The fact is that the gospel about Jesus and the gospel of Jesus are the same. The gospel that Jesus proclaimed was a gospel about Him. It was a gospel that offered Him as Saviour. It was a gospel that told the good news of His saving work.

He proclaimed that gospel even during His earthly ministry. He offered Himself even then as Saviour. He pointed forward to His atoning death on the cross and to His glorious resurrection. Then, when He had died and risen again, when His redeeming work was done, He told the story of it through the apostles whom He had chosen and through the Holy Spirit whom He sent.

Let us get this thing perfectly straight. Let us not be afraid of repeating it. *Jesus is both the author and the substance of the gospel.* Jesus died for our sins on the cross. The story of His death and of the things that go with it is the gospel. It is the good news. But after Jesus had died and risen again, did He leave it to others to bring that good news to us? Not at all! He brought us the good news Himself.

That is what we mean by saying that when we study now the work of Jesus as a priest, we are not belittling or turning away from His work as a prophet. On the contrary we are just listening to what Jesus as a prophet so graciously tells us about Himself. As a prophet Jesus tells us the story of His priestly work. As a prophet He tells us about the way in which, as the one true priest, He offered Himself once for all as a sacrifice to satisfy divine justice and reconcile us to God, and He tells us about the way in which He is now continually making intercession for us.

Let us hear, then, what Jesus Himself tells us about His priestly work. Let us hear it as it is contained in the whole Bible from Genesis to Revelation.

A priest, we observed in the last talk, is a representative of men in the presence of God. He is a mediator between God and men. He obtains access for men unto God.

Do we need a priest, in that sense of the word? That is the first question. If we do not need a priest at all, then of course all this talk about the priestly work of Christ is without practical importance. If we, in our own right, already have access to God, then we have no need that Christ should enter for us within the veil.

A great many people today take exactly that view of the matter. We are, they say, already children of God, by virtue of the fact that we are men; we already have free access to God. All we need is to overcome our fear of God; all that we need is to have presented to us the great truth that God is our Father.

Jesus, they say, has presented that great truth to us, and for that we revere Him. He was the first man to make full use of the privilege which man has as man – the privilege of standing before God without fear, as a child stands before a loving father. Following Jesus we can make use of the same privilege. But that does not mean in the slightest that Jesus is a priest whose intermediation is necessary in order that we may approach God. On the contrary, the thing that Jesus discovered was just the comforting fact that no intermediation was necessary – neither His nor anyone else's. He led the way, and we follow. But we follow in our own right, and we could have led the way ourselves if only we had had the courage. Jesus merely encouraged us to make use of a privilege which was already ours.

That is the way of looking at the matter that dominates most of the nominally Christian churches of the present day. But it is radically contrary to the Bible, and it must be radically rejected by all those who believe the Bible to be truly the Word of God.

According to the Bible all mankind, since the fall, is under the just condemnation of God's law, subject to God's wrath and curse, utterly unable to do any good. All mankind, in other words, is lost in sin. Being lost in sin, men have no right of access unto God. On the contrary they are separated from God by a flaming sword. They are under the awful penalty of God's law, and if that penalty is treated as though it did not exist, God ceases to be God and evil has triumphed over good.

That, my friends, is the situation of fallen man. It is not presented to us just in one part of the Bible. It is presented to us in the whole Bible. From the first book of the Bible to the last, the Bible beats down men's pagan optimism; it opposes the central article of the pagan creed, which is the article: 'I believe in man.' It takes from us the last vestige of confidence that in ourselves we have any right of access unto God; it teaches us to fear the righteous God, and to stand in terror before the majesty of His offended law.

It teaches us, therefore, that if we are to have any access unto God, it can only be through a priest. The priest must be one of us, since He is to be our representative; but He must also be more than merely one of us. If He were merely one of us, He would have no more right of access unto God than we have. Like us He would be a sinner, subject to God's wrath and curse. But even if He were sinless, still if He were merely man He could not possibly bring us to God. Any sacrifice that He might offer for us, any punishment that He might endure for a time in our stead, would, if He were merely man, have at best only a finite value. It could

174

not possibly be accepted instead of the eternal punishment which was the just penalty of the law upon our sin.

If we are to have truly a priest who can bring us to God, it can only be one who is both man and God – man that He might suffer in our stead, God that His suffering in our stead might have worth enough to satisfy the law's demands.

Such a priest, such an high priest, thank God, we have. It is Christ Jesus the Lord. He was, from all eternity, God. Through Him the worlds were made. For one purpose did He humble Himself; for one purpose did He become man – that He might be our priest to reconcile us to God, that He might offer on the cross for us sinners a perfect sacrifice to fulfil the law's demands and wipe out the dread handwriting that was against us. Through Him and Him alone we come to God; through His constant intercession alone do we stand in God's presence. In our own right we deserve only to be cast out from God's presence and suffer to all eternity the just punishment of sin. In Him alone we enter without fear unto the throne of God – not God's children in our own right but made God's children through the precious blood of Christ.

What a joy it is to search the Scriptures ever anew to see what God has told us in His Word concerning that priestly work of Christ! It is folly indeed to the men of the world; no pursuit seems to them to be more futile. What time have we, they say, to engage in these theological subtleties? But to the sinner saved by grace how sweet a thing it is to contemplate the cross of Christ! How sweet a thing it is to follow the doctrine of the shed blood that runs like a red cord through the Bible from Genesis to Revelation! How sweet a thing it is to trace the gradual unfolding of the promise from the time when sin first entered into the world! How sweet a thing it is to behold the fulfilling of the promise in those strangely simple narratives in Matthew, Mark,

Luke and John! How sweet a thing it is to explore the divine explanation of the fulfilment in the epistles of Paul! How sweet a thing it is to follow the directions there given as the Spirit applies to us the benefits of what our Saviour did! How sweet a thing it is to contemplate the unity of the sacred Book as it finds its centre in the cross!

May that joy, my friends, be ours as we study the cross of Christ together on these Sunday afternoons! And as we have that joy, may we also have the joy of bringing others with us to the foot of the cross. May God grant that some who listen to these expositions of the Word, and who have not yet found Jesus as their Saviour, may find Him as He is presented to them in the Word of God!

Are you weary and heavy laden? Are you tired of a life of sin? Are you dissatisfied with the world's righteousness which is no righteousness in God's sight? Have you some dread vision of the majesty of God's offended law? Oh, then will you not come to Him who can give you rest? Will you not drink of the water of salvation? Will you not trust Him who died for you?

Ah, salvation is so near! To have it you do not need to ascend into the heights or descend into the abyss:

> But the righteousness which is of faith speaketh on this wise, Say not in thine heart, Who shall ascend into heaven? (that is, to bring Christ down from above:) or, Who shall descend into the deep? (that is, to bring up Christ again from the dead.) But what saith it? The word is nigh thee, even in thy mouth, and in thy heart: that is, the word of faith, which we preach; that if thou shalt confess with thy mouth the Lord Jesus, and shalt believe in thine heart that God hath raised Him from the dead, thou shalt be saved (Rom. 10:6-9).

May the Lord Jesus Christ, the risen Saviour, attend through His Spirit the message of His cross, that precious souls may be saved!

# 18: *The Doctrine of the Atonement*

THE priestly work of Christ, or at least that part of it in which He offered Himself up as a sacrifice to satisfy divine justice and reconcile us to God, is commonly called the atonement, and the doctrine which sets it forth is commonly called the doctrine of the atonement. That doctrine is at the very heart of what is taught in the Word of God.

Before we present that doctrine, we ought to observe that the term by which it is ordinarily designated is not altogether free from objection.

When I say that the term 'atonement' is open to objection, I am not referring to the fact that it occurs only once in the King James Version of the New Testament, and is therefore, so far as New Testament usage is concerned, not a common Biblical term. A good many other terms which are rare in the Bible are nevertheless admirable terms when one comes to summarise Biblical teaching. As a matter of fact this term is rather common in the Old Testament (though it occurs only that once in the New Testament), but that fact would not be necessary to commend it if it were satisfactory in other ways. Even if it were not common in either Testament it still might be exactly the term for us to use to designate by one word what the Bible teaches in a number of words.

The real objection to it is of an entirely different kind. It is a twofold objection. The word 'atonement,' in the first place, is ambiguous, and in the second place, it is not broad enough.

The one place where the word occurs in the King

James Version of the New Testament is Romans 5:11, where Paul says:

> *And not only so, but we also joy in God through our Lord Jesus Christ, by whom we have now received the atonement.*

Here the word is used to translate a Greek word meaning 'reconciliation.' This usage seems to be very close to the etymological meaning of the word, for it does seem to be true that the English word 'atonement' means 'at-onement.' It is, therefore, according to its derivation, a natural word to designate the state of reconciliation between two parties formerly at variance.

In the Old Testament, on the other hand, where the word occurs in the King James Version not once, but forty or fifty times, it has a different meaning; it has the meaning of 'propitiation.' Thus we read in Leviticus 1:4, regarding a man who brings a bullock to be killed as a burnt offering:

> *And he shall put his hand upon the head of the burnt offering; and it shall be accepted for him to make atonement for him.*

So also the word occurs some eight times in the King James Version in the sixteenth chapter of Leviticus, where the provisions of the law are set forth regarding the great day of atonement. Take, for example, the following verses in that chapter:

> *And Aaron shall offer his bullock of the sin offering, which is for himself, and make an atonement for himself, and for his house* (Lev. 16:6).
> *Then shall he kill the goat of the sin offering that is for the people, and bring his blood within the veil, and do with that blood as he did with the blood of the bullock, and sprinkle it upon the mercy seat:*
> *And he shall make atonement for the holy place, because of the uncleanness of the children of Israel, and because of their transgressions in all their sins: and so shall he do for*

*the tabernacle of the congregation, that remaineth among them in the midst of their uncleanness* (Lev. 16:15f.).

In these passages the meaning of the word is clear. God has been offended because of the sins of the people or of individuals among His people. The priest kills the animal which is brought as a sacrifice. God is thereby propitiated, and those who have offended God are forgiven.

I am not now asking whether those Old Testament sacrifices brought forgiveness in themselves, or merely as prophecies of a greater sacrifice to come; I am not now considering the significant limitations which the Old Testament law attributes to their efficacy. We shall try to deal with those matters in some subsequent talk. All that I am here interested in is the use of the word 'atonement' in the English Bible. All that I am saying is that that word in the Old Testament clearly conveys the notion of something that is done to satisfy God in order that the sins of men may be forgiven and their communion with God restored.

Somewhat akin to this Old Testament use of the word 'atonement' is the use of it in our everyday parlance where religion is not at all in view. Thus we often say that someone in his youth was guilty of a grievous fault but has fully 'atoned' for it or made full 'atonement' for it by a long and useful life. We mean by that that the person in question has – if we may use a colloquial phrase – 'made up for' his youthful indiscretion by his subsequent life of usefulness and rectitude. Mind you, I am not at all saying that a man can really 'make up for' or 'atone for' a youthful sin by a subsequent life of usefulness and rectitude; but I am just saying that that indicates the way in which the English word is used. In our ordinary usage the word certainly conveys the idea of something like compensation for some wrong that has been done.

It certainly conveys that notion also in those Old

Testament passages. Of course that is not the only notion that it conveys in those passages. There the use of the word is very much more specific. The compensation which is indicated by the word is a compensation rendered to God, and it is a compensation that has become necessary because of an offence committed against God. Still, the notion of compensation or satisfaction is clearly in the word. God is offended because of sin; satisfaction is made to Him in some way by the sacrifice; and so His favour is restored.

Thus in the English Bible the word 'atonement' is used in two rather distinct senses. In its one occurrence in the New Testament it designates the particular means by which such reconciliation is effected – namely, the sacrifice which God is pleased to accept in order that man may again be received into favour.

Now of these two uses of the word it is unquestionably the Old Testament use which is followed when we speak of the 'doctrine of the atonement.' We mean by the word, when we thus use it in theology, not the reconciliation between God and man, not the 'at-one-ment' between God and man, but specifically the means by which that reconciliation is effected – namely, the death of Christ as something that was necessary in order that sinful man might be received into communion with God.

I do not see any great objection to the use of the word in that way – provided only that we are perfectly clear that we are using it in that way. Certainly it has acquired too firm a place in Christian theology and has gathered around it too many precious associations for us to think, now, of trying to dislodge it.

However, there is another word which would in itself have been much better, and it is really a great pity that it has not come into more general use in this connection. That is the word 'satisfaction.' If we only had acquired the habit of saying that Christ made full satisfaction to God for man that would have conveyed a more adequate account of Christ's priestly work as our Redeemer than the word 'atonement' can convey. It designates what the word 'atonement' – rightly understood – designates, and it also designates something more. We shall see what that something more is in a subsequent talk.

But it is time now for us to enter definitely into our great subject. Men were estranged from God by sin; Christ as their great high priest has brought them back into communion with God. How has He done so? That is the question with which we shall be dealing in a number of the talks that now follow.

This afternoon all that I can do is to try to state the Scripture doctrine in bare summary (or begin to state it), leaving it to subsequent talks to show how that Scripture doctrine is actually taught in the Scriptures, to defend it against objections, and to distinguish it clearly from various unscriptural theories.

What then in bare outline does the Bible teach about the 'atonement'? What does it teach – to use a better term – about the satisfaction which Christ presented to God in order that sinful man might be received into God's favour?

I cannot possibly answer this question even in bare summary unless I call your attention to the Biblical doctrine of sin with which we dealt last winter. You cannot possibly understand what the Bible says about salvation unless you understand what the Bible says about the thing from which we are saved.

If then we ask what is the Biblical doctrine of sin, we observe, in the first place, that according to the Bible all men are sinners.

Well, then, that being so, it becomes important to ask what this sin is which has affected all mankind. Is it just an excusable imperfection; is it something that can be transcended as a man can transcend the immaturity of his youthful years? Or, supposing it to be more than imperfection, supposing it to be something like a

181

definite stain, is it a stain that can easily be removed as writing is erased from a slate?

The Bible leaves us in no doubt as to the answer to these questions. Sin, it tells us, is disobedience to the law of God, and the law of God is entirely irrevocable.

Why is the law of God irrevocable? The Bible makes that plain. Because it is rooted in the nature of God! God is righteous and that is the reason why His law is righteous. Can He then revoke His law or allow it to be disregarded? Well, there is of course no external compulsion upon Him to prevent Him from doing these things. There is none who can say to Him, 'What doest thou?' In that sense He can do all things. But the point is, He cannot revoke His law and still remain God. He cannot, without Himself becoming unrighteous, make His law either forbid righteousness or condone unrighteousness. When the law of God says, 'The soul that sinneth it shall die,' that awful penalty of death is, indeed, imposed by God's will; but God's will is determined by God's nature, and God's nature being unchangeably holy the penalty must run its course. God would be untrue to Himself, in other words, if sin were not punished; and that God should be untrue to Himself is the most impossible thing that can possibly be conceived.

Under that majestic law of God man was placed in the estate wherein he was created. Man was placed in a probation, which theologians call the covenant of works. If he obeyed the law during a certain limited period, his probation was to be over; he would be given eternal life without any further possibility of loss. If, on the other hand, he disobeyed the law, he would have death – physical death and eternal death in hell.

Man entered into that probation with every advantage. He was created in knowledge, righteousness and holiness. He was created not merely neutral with respect to goodness; he was created positively good. Yet he fell. He failed to make his goodness an assured and

eternal goodness; he failed to progress from the goodness of innocency to the confirmed goodness which
would have been the reward for standing the test. He
transgressed the commandment of God, and so came
under the awful curse of the law.

Under that curse came all mankind. That covenant
of works had been made with the first man, Adam, not
only for himself but for his posterity. He had stood, in
that probation, in a representative capacity; he had
stood – to use a better terminology – as the federal head
of the race, having been made the federal head of the
race by divine appointment. If he had successfully met
the test, all mankind descended from him would have
been born in a state of confirmed righteousness and
blessedness, without any possibility of falling into sin
or of losing eternal life. But as a matter of fact Adam
did not successfully meet the test. He transgressed the
commandment of God, and since he was the federal
head, the divinely appointed representative of the race,
all mankind sinned in him and fell with him in his first
transgression.

Thus all mankind, descended from Adam by ordinary
generation, are themselves under the dreadful penalty
of the law of God. They are under that penalty at birth,
before they have done anything either good or bad. Part
of that penalty is the want of the righteousness with
which man was created, and a dreadful corruption
which is called original sin. Proceeding from that
corruption when men grow to years of discretion come
individual acts of transgression.

Can the penalty of sin resting upon all mankind be
remitted? Plainly not, if God is to remain God. That
penalty of sin was ordained in the law of God, and the
law of God was no mere arbitrary and changeable
arrangement but an expression of the nature of God
Himself. If the penalty of sin were remitted, God would
become unrighteous, and that God will not become

unrighteous is the most certain thing that can possibly be conceived.

How then can sinful men be saved? In one way only. Only if a substitute is provided who shall pay for them the just penalty of God's law.

The Bible teaches that such a substitute has as a matter of fact been provided. The substitute is Jesus Christ. The law's demands of penalty must be satisfied. There is no escaping that. But Jesus Christ satisfied those demands for us when He died instead of us on the cross.

I have used the word 'satisfied' advisedly. It is very important for us to observe that when Jesus died upon the cross He made a full satisfaction for our sins; He paid the penalty which the law pronounces upon our sin, not in part but in full.

In saying that, there are several misunderstandings which need to be guarded against in the most careful possible way. Only by distinguishing the Scripture doctrine carefully from several distortions of it can we understand clearly what the Scripture doctrine is. I want to point out, therefore, several things that we do not mean when we say that Christ paid the penalty of our sin by dying instead of us on the cross.

In the first place, we do not mean that when Christ took our place He became Himself a sinner. Of course He did not become a sinner. Never was His glorious righteousness and goodness more wonderfully seen than when He bore the curse of God's law upon the cross. He was not deserving of that curse. Far from it! He was deserving of all praise.

What we mean, therefore, when we say that Christ bore our guilt is not that He became guilty, but that He paid the penalty that we so richly deserved.

In the second place, we do not mean that Christ's sufferings were the same as the sufferings that we should have endured if we had paid the penalty of our own sins. Obviously they were not the same. Part of the sufferings that we should have endured would have been the dreadful suffering of remorse. Christ did not endure that suffering, for He had done no wrong. Moreover, our sufferings would have endured to all eternity, whereas Christ's sufferings on the cross endured but a few hours. Plainly then His sufferings were not the same as ours would have been.

In the third place, however, an opposite error must also be warded off. If Christ's sufferings were not the same as ours, it is also quite untrue to say that He paid only a part of the penalty that was due to us because of our sin. Some theologians have fallen into that error. When man incurred the penalty of the law, they have said, God was pleased to take some other and lesser thing – namely, the sufferings of Christ on the cross – instead of exacting the full penalty. Thus, according to these theologians, the demands of the law were not really satisfied by the death of Christ, but God was simply pleased, in arbitrary fashion, to accept something less than full satisfaction.

That is a very serious error indeed. Instead of falling into it we shall, if we are true to the Scriptures, insist that Christ on the cross paid the full and just penalty for our sin.

The error arose because of a confusion between the payment of a debt and the payment of a penalty. In the case of a debt it does not make any difference who pays; all that is essential is that the creditor shall receive what is owed him. What is essential is that just the same thing shall be paid as that which stood in the bond.

But in the case of the payment of a penalty it does make a difference who pays. The law demanded that we should suffer eternal death because of our sin. Christ paid the penalty of the law in our stead. But for Him to suffer was not the same as for us to suffer. He is God, and not merely man. Therefore if He had suffered to all eternity as we should have suffered, that would not have been to pay the just penalty of the sin, but it would have been an unjust exaction of vastly more. In other words, we must get rid of merely quantitative notions in thinking of the sufferings of Christ. What He suffered on the cross was what the law of God truly demanded not of any person but of such a person as Himself when He became our substitute in paying the penalty of sin. He did therefore make full and not merely partial satisfaction for the claims of the law against us.

Finally, it is very important to observe that the Bible's teaching about the cross of Christ does not mean that God waited for someone else to pay the penalty of sin before He would forgive the sinner. So unbelievers constantly represent it, but that representation is radically wrong. No, God Himself paid the penalty of sin – God Himself in the Person of God the Son, who loved us and gave Himself for us, God Himself in the person of God the Father who so loved the world as to give His only-begotten Son, God the Holy Spirit who applies to us the benefits of Christ's death. God's the cost and ours the marvellous gain! Who shall measure the depths of the love of God which was extended to us sinners when the Lord Jesus took our place and died in our stead upon the accursed tree?

# 19: *The Active Obedience of Christ*

LAST Sunday afternoon, in outlining the Biblical teaching about the work of Christ in satisfying for us the claims of God's law, I said nothing about one very important part of that work. I pointed out that Christ by His death in our stead on the cross paid the just penalty of our sin, but I said nothing of another thing that He did for us. I said nothing about what Christ did for us by His active obedience to God's law. It is very important that we should fill out that part of the outline before we go one step further.

Suppose Christ had done for us merely what we said last Sunday afternoon that He did. Suppose He had merely paid the just penalty of the law that was resting upon us for our sin, and had done nothing more than that; where would we then be? Well, I think we can say – if indeed it is legitimate to separate one part of the work of Christ even in thought from the rest – that if Christ had merely paid the penalty of sin for us and had done nothing more we should be at best back in the situation in which Adam found himself when God placed him under the covenant of works.

That covenant of works was a probation. If Adam kept the law of God for a certain period, he was to have eternal life. If he disobeyed he was to have death. Well, he disobeyed, and the penalty of death was inflicted upon him and his posterity. Then Christ by His death on the cross paid that penalty for those whom God had chosen.

Well and good. But if that were all that Christ did for us, do you not see that we should be back in just the situation in which Adam was before he sinned? The penalty of his sinning would have been removed from us because it had all been paid by Christ. But for the future the attainment of eternal life would have been dependent upon our perfect obedience to the law of God. We should simply have been back in the probation again.

Moreover, we should have been back in that probation in a very much less hopeful way than that in which Adam was originally placed in it. Everything was in Adam's favour when he was placed in the probation. He had been created in knowledge, righteousness and holiness. He had been created positively good. Yet despite all that, he fell. How much more likely would we be to fall – nay, how certain to fall – if all that Christ had done for us were merely to remove from us the guilt of past sin, leaving it then to our own efforts to win the reward which God has pronounced upon perfect obedience!

But I really must decline to speculate any further about what might have been if Christ had done something less for us than that which He has actually done. As a matter of fact, He has not merely paid the penalty of Adam's first sin, and the penalty of the sins which we individually have committed, but also He has positively merited for us eternal life. He was, in other words, our representative both in penalty paying and in probation keeping. He paid the penalty of sin for us, and He stood the probation for us.

That is the reason why those who have been saved by the Lord Jesus Christ are in a far more blessed condition than was Adam before he fell. Adam before he fell was righteous in the sight of God, but he was still under the possibility of becoming unrighteous. Those who have been saved by the Lord Jesus Christ not only are righteous in the sight of God but they are beyond the possibility of becoming unrighteous. In their case, the probation is over. It is not over because they have stood it successfully. It is not over because they have themselves earned the reward of assured blessedness which God promised on condition of perfect obedience. But it is over because Christ has stood it for them; it is over because Christ has merited for them the reward by His perfect obedience to God's law.

I think I can make the matter plain if I imagine a dialogue between the law of God and a sinful man saved by grace.

'Man,' says the law of God, 'have you obeyed my commands?'

'No,' says the sinner saved by grace. 'I have disobeyed them, not only in the person of my representative Adam in his first sin, but also in that I myself have sinned in thought, word and deed.'

'Well, then, sinner,' says the law of God, 'have you paid the penalty which I pronounced upon disobedience?'

'No,' says the sinner, 'I have not paid the penalty myself; but Christ has paid it for me. He was my representative when He died there on the cross. Hence, so far as the penalty is concerned, I am clear.'

'Well, then, sinner,' says the law of God, 'how about the conditions which God has pronounced for the attainment of assured blessedness? Have you stood the test? Have you merited eternal life by perfect obedience during the period of probation?'

'No,' says the sinner, 'I have not merited eternal life by my own perfect obedience. God knows and my own conscience knows that even after I became a Christian I have sinned in thought, word and deed. But although I have not merited eternal life by any obedience of my own, Christ has merited it for me by His perfect obedience. He was not for Himself subject to the law. No obedience was required of Him for Himself, since He was Lord of all. That obedience, then, which He rendered to the law when He was on earth was rendered by Him as my representative. I have no righteousness of my own, but clad in Christ's perfect righteousness, imputed to me and received by faith alone, I can glory in the fact that so far as I am concerned the probation has been kept and as God is true there awaits me the glorious reward which Christ thus earned for me.'

Such, put in bald, simple form, is the dialogue between every Christian and the law of God. How gloriously complete is the salvation wrought for us by Christ! Christ paid the penalty, and He merited the reward. Those are the two great things that He has done for us.

Theologians are accustomed to distinguish those two parts of the saving work of Christ by calling one of them His passive obedience and the other of them His active obedience. By His passive obedience – that is, by suffering in our stead – He paid the penalty for us; by His active obedience – that is, by doing what the law of God required – He has merited for us the reward.

I like that terminology well enough. I think it does set forth as well as can be done in human language the two aspects of Christ's work. And yet a danger lurks in it if it leads us to think that one of the two parts of Christ's work can be separated from the other.

How shall we distinguish Christ's active obedience from His passive obedience? Shall we say that He accomplished His active obedience by His life and accomplished His passive obedience by His death? No, that will not do at all. During every moment of His life upon earth Christ was engaged in His passive obedience. It was all for Him humiliation, was it not? It was all suffering. It was all part of His payment of the penalty of sin. On the other hand, we cannot say that His death was passive obedience and not active obedience. On the contrary, His death was the crown of His active obedience. It was the crown of that obedience to the law of God by which He merited eternal life for those whom He came to save.

Do you not see, then, what the true state of the case is? Christ's active obedience and His passive obedience are not two divisions of His work, some of the events of His earthly life being His active obedience and other events of His life being His passive obedience; but every event of His life was both active obedience and passive obedience. Every event of His life was a part of His payment of the penalty of sin, and every event of His life was a part of that glorious keeping of the law of God by which He earned for His people the reward of eternal life. The two aspects of His work, in other words, are inextricably intertwined. Neither was performed apart from the other. Together they constitute the wonderful, full salvation which was wrought for us by Christ our Redeemer.

We can put it briefly by saying that Christ took our place with respect to the law of God. He paid for us the law's penalty, and He obeyed for us the law's commands. He saved us from hell, and He earned for us our entrance into heaven. All that we have, then, we owe unto Him. There is no blessing that we have in this world or the next for which we should not give Christ thanks.

As I say that, I am fully conscious of the inadequacy of my words. I have tried to summarise the teaching of the Bible about the saving work of Christ; yet how cold and dry seems any mere human summary – even if it were far better than mine – in comparison with the marvellous richness and warmth of the Bible itself. It is to the Bible itself that I am going to ask you to turn with me next Sunday afternoon. Having tried to summarise the Bible's teaching in order that we may take each part of the Bible in proper relation to other parts, I am going to ask you next Sunday to turn with me to the great texts themselves, in order that we may test our summary, and every human summary, by what God Himself has told us in His Word. Ah, when we do that, what refreshment it is to our souls! How infinitely superior is God's Word to all human attempts to summarise its teaching! Those attempts are necessary;

we could not do without them; everyone who is really true to the Bible will engage in them. But it is the very words of the Bible that touch the heart, and everything that we – or for the matter of that even the great theologians – say in summary of the Bible must be compared ever anew with the Bible itself.

This afternoon, however, just in order that next Sunday we may begin our searching of the Scriptures in the most intelligent possible way, I am going to ask you to glance with me at one or two of the different views that men have held regarding the cross of Christ.

I have already summarised for you the orthodox view. According to that view, Christ took our place on the cross, paying the penalty of sin that we deserved to pay. That view can be put in very simple language. We deserved eternal death because of sin; Jesus, because He loved us, took our place and died in our stead on the cross. Call that view repulsive if you will. It is indeed repulsive to the natural man. But do not call it difficult to understand. A little child can understand it, and can receive it to the salvation of his soul.

Rejecting that substitutionary view, many men have advanced other views. Many are the theories of the atonement. Yet I do think that their bewildering variety may be reduced to something like order if we observe that they fall into a very few general divisions.

Most common among them is the theory that Christ's death upon the cross had merely a moral effect upon man. Man is by nature a child of God, say the advocates of that view. But unfortunately he is not making full use of his high privilege. He has fallen into terrible degradation, and having fallen into terrible degradation he has become estranged from God. He no longer lives in that intimate relationship of sonship with God in which he ought to live.

How shall this estrangement between man and God be removed; how shall man be brought back into fellowship with God? Why, say the advocates of the view of which we are now speaking, simply by inducing man to turn from his evil ways and make full use of his high privilege as a child of God. There is certainly no barrier on God's side; the only barrier lies in man's foolish and wicked heart. Once overcome that barrier and all will be well. Once touch man's stony heart so that he will come to see again that God is his Father, once lead him also to overcome any fear of God as though God were not always more ready to forgive than man is to be forgiven; and at once the true relationship between God and man can be restored and man can go forward joyously to the use, in holy living, of his high privilege as a child of the loving heavenly Father.

But how can man's heart be touched, that he may be led to return to his Father's house and live as befits a son of God? By the contemplation of the cross of Christ, say the advocates of the view that we are now presenting. Jesus Christ was truly a son of God. Indeed, He was a son of God in such a unique way that He may be called in some sort *the* Son of God. When therefore God gave Him to die upon the cross and when He willingly gave Himself to die, that was a wonderful manifestation of God's love for sinning, erring humanity. In the presence of that love all opposition in man's heart should be broken down. He should recognise at last the fact that God is indeed his Father, and recognising that, he should make use of his high privilege of living the life that befits a child of God.

Such is the so-called 'moral-influence theory' of the atonement. It is held in a thousand different forms, and it is held by thousands of people who have not the slightest notion that they are holding it.

Some of those who have held it have tried to maintain with it something like a real belief in the deity of Christ. If Christ was really the eternal Son of God, then the gift of Him on the cross becomes all the greater evidence of the love of God. But the overwhelming majority of those who hold the moral-influence view of the atonement have given up all real belief in the deity of Christ. These persons hold simply that Jesus on the cross gave us a supreme example of self-sacrifice. By that example we are inspired to do likewise. We are inspired to sacrifice our lives, either in actual martyrdom in some holy cause or in sacrificial service. Sacrificing thus our lives, we discover that we have thereby attained a higher life than ever before. Thus the cross of Christ has been the pathway that leads us to moral heights.

Read most of the popular books on religion of the present day, and then tell me whether you do not think that that is at bottom what they mean. Some of them speak about the cross of Christ. Some of them say that Christ's sufferings were redemptive. But the trouble is they hold that the cross of Christ is not merely Christ's cross but our cross; and that while Christ's sufferings were redemptive our sufferings are redemptive too. All they really mean is that Christ on Calvary pointed out a way that we follow. He hallowed the pathway of self-sacrifice. We follow in that path and thus we obtain a higher life for our souls.

That is the great central and all-pervading vice of most modern books that deal with the cross. They make the cross of Christ merely an example of a general principle of self-sacrifice. And if they talk still of salvation, they tell us that we are saved by walking in the way of the cross. It is thus, according to this view, not Christ's cross but our cross that saves us. The way of the cross leads us to God. Christ may have a great influence in leading us to walk in that way of the cross, that way of self-sacrifice; but it is our walking in it and not Christ's walking in it which really saves us. Thus we are saved by our own efforts, not by Christ's blood after all. It is the same old notion that sinful man can save himself. It is that notion just decked out in new garments and making use of Christian terminology.

Such is the moral-influence theory of the atonement.

In addition to it, we find what is sometimes called the governmental theory. What a strange, compromising, tortuous thing that governmental theory is, to be sure!

According to the governmental view, the death of Christ was not necessary in order that any eternal justice of God, rooted in the divine nature, might be satisfied. So far the governmental view goes with the advocates of the moral-influence theory. But, it holds, the death of Christ was necessary in order that good discipline might be maintained in the world. If sinners were allowed to get the notion that sin could go altogether unpunished, there would be no adequate deterrent from sin. Being thus undeterred from sin, men would go on sinning and the world would be thrown into confusion. But if the world were thus thrown into moral confusion that would not be for the best interests of the greatest number. Therefore God held up the death of Christ on the cross as an indication of how serious a thing sin is, so that men may be deterred from sinning and so order in the world may be preserved.

Having thus indicated – so the governmental theory runs – how serious a thing sin is, God proceeded to offer salvation to men on easier terms than those on which He had originally offered it. He had originally offered it on the basis of perfect obedience. Now He offered it on the basis of faith. He could safely offer it on those easier terms, and He could safely remit the penalty originally pronounced upon sin, because in the awful spectacle of the cross of Christ He had sufficiently indicated to men that sin is a serious offence and that if it is committed something or other has to be done about the matter in order that the good order of the universe may be conserved.

Such is the governmental theory. But do you not see that really at bottom it is just a form of the moral-influence theory? Like the moral-influence theory, it holds that the only obstacle to fellowship between man and God is found in man's will. Like the moral-influence theory it denies that there is any eternal justice of God, rooted in His being, and it denies that the eternal justice of God demands the punishment of sin. Like the moral-influence theory it plays fast and loose with God's holiness, and like the moral-influence theory, we may add, it loses sight of the real depths of God's love. No man who holds the light view of sin that is involved in these man-made theories has the slightest notion of what it cost when the eternal Son of God took our place upon the accursed tree.

People sometimes say, indeed, that it makes little difference what theory of the atonement we may hold. Ah, my friends, it makes all the difference in the world. When you contemplate the cross of Christ, do you say merely, with modern theorists, 'What a noble example of self-sacrifice; I am going to attain favour with God by sacrificing myself as well as He.' Or do you say with the Bible, 'He loved me and gave Himself for me; He took my place; He bore my curse; He bought me with His own most precious blood.' That is the most momentous question that can come to any human soul. I want you all to turn with me next Sunday afternoon to the Word of God in order that we may answer that question aright.

# 20: *The Bible and the Cross*

HAVING observed last week what are the leading views that have been held regarding the cross of Christ, we turn now to the Bible in order to discover which of these views is right.

Did Jesus on the cross really take our place, paying the penalty of God's law which justly rested upon us? That is the orthodox or substitutionary view of the atonement.

Or did He merely exert a good moral influence upon us by His death, either by giving us an exhibition of the love of God or by inspiring us to sacrifice our lives for the welfare of others as He sacrificed Himself? That is the so-called moral-influence theory of the atonement.

Or did He by His death merely conserve the good discipline of the world by showing that, in the interests of the welfare of the greatest number, God cannot simply allow His law to be transgressed with complete impunity? That is the so-called governmental theory of the atonement.

We shall try to test these three views of the cross of Christ by comparing them with what the Bible actually says. But before we do so, there are two preliminary remarks that we ought to make.

Our first remark is that the three views of the atonement really reduce themselves to two. Both the moral-influence and the governmental view of the atonement really make the work of Christ terminate upon man, rather than upon God. They both proceed on the assumption that, in order that man shall be forgiven, nothing but man's repentance is required. They both of them deny, at least by implication, that there is such a thing as an eternal principle of justice, not based merely upon the interests of the creature but rooted in the nature of God – an eternal principle of justice demanding that sin shall be punished. They both of them favour the notion that the ethical attributes of God may be summed up in the one attribute – benevolence. They both of them tend to distort the great Scriptural assertion that 'God is love' into the very different assertion that God is *nothing but love*. They both of them tend to find the supreme end of the creation in the happiness or well-being of the creature. They both of them fail utterly to attain to any high notion of the awful holiness of God.

No doubt the governmental theory disguises these tendencies more than the moral-influence theory does. It does show some recognition of the moral chaos which would result if men got the notion that the law of God could be transgressed with complete impunity.

But, after all, even the governmental theory denies that there is any real underlying necessity for the punishment of sin. Punishment, it holds, is merely remedial and deterrent. It is intended merely to prevent future sin, not to expiate past sin. So the tragedy on Calvary, according to the advocates of the governmental view, was intended by God merely to shock sinners out of their complacency; it was intended merely to show what terrible effects sin has so that sinners by observing those terrible effects might be led to stop sinning. The governmental view, therefore, like the moral-influence view, has at its centre the notion that a moral effect exerted upon man was the sole purpose of the cross of Christ.

Very different is the substitutionary view. According to that view, not a mere moral effect upon man but the satisfaction of the eternal justice of God was the primary end for which Christ died. Hence the substitutionary view of the atonement stands sharply over against the other two. The other two belong in one category; the substitutionary view belongs in an entirely different category. That is the first remark that we desire to make before we begin to consider the Biblical teaching in detail.

That remark, however, would be decidedly misleading unless we went on to make a second remark. Our second remark is that the substitutionary view of the atonement, though it makes the work of Christ in dying upon the cross terminate primarily upon God, yet does at the same time most emphatically make it terminate also upon man. What a distortion of the substitutionary view it would be to say that Christ, when He died, did not die to produce a moral effect upon man!

Of course He died to produce a moral effect upon man! If He had not died, man would have continued to lead a life of sin; but as it is, those for whom He died cease to lead a life of sin and begin to lead a life of holiness. They do not lead that life of holiness perfectly in this world, but they will most certainly lead it in the world to come, and it was in order that they might lead that life of holiness that Christ died for them. No man for whom Christ died continues to live in sin as he lived before. All who receive the benefits of the cross of Christ turn from sin unto righteousness. In holding that that is the case, the substitutionary view of the atonement is quite in accord with the moral-influence theory and with the governmental theory.

Well, then, is it correct to say that the moral-influence theory and the governmental theory are correct as far as they go and merely differ from the substitutionary view in being inadequate or incomplete?

No, I do not think that that is correct at all. You see, the heart and core of the moral-influence theory and the governmental theory is found in the denial that Christ on the cross took our place and paid the just penalty of our sins that we might be right with God. Denying that, the moral-influence theory and the governmental theory are, if the substitutionary view is right, not merely inadequate but also false.

Moreover, the moral-influence theory and the governmental theory are not even right in what they affirm, to say nothing of their being right in what they deny. They are indeed right in holding that Christ died to bring about a moral change in men, but they are wrong in thinking that that moral change can be brought about if the moral-influence theory or the governmental theory is true. They are wrong in not observing clearly that fallen man, dead in trespasses and sins, can never be made to live a holy life merely by the introduction of new motives or new incentives to goodness, but only by the new birth which is the work of the Spirit of God. They are wrong in not observing that that new birth, which is the necessary prerequisite for any living of a holy life by fallen man, is part of the benefit purchased by Christ when He died on the cross to make sinners right with God by His payment, for them, of the penalty of sin.

I do not mean that all of the advocates of the moral-influence theory or the governmental theory of the atonement deny the necessity of the new birth, but I do mean that the denial of it is part of the logical implications of their views. If Christ died on the cross merely to bring to bear a good moral influence upon men, then it does look as though a good moral influence is all that men really need; and if a good moral influence is all that they need, then it does look as though Jesus was wrong when He said, 'Ye must be born again.'

Moreover, how feeble is the moral influence exerted by the cross if the cross of Christ is only what the advocates of the moral-influence theory suppose it to be! If Jesus' death on Calvary was merely a sort of exhibition of the love of God, not necessary in itself but merely necessary in order that our hearts may be touched and we may be moved to salutary tears, then, the moment we find out that that was all it was, it seems to me our tears of repentance are apt to be dried up. It is as though we had sat in some playhouse witnessing some heart-moving tragedy, entering into the struggles of the characters on the stage, imagining that it was all real. But then the curtain has fallen, and out we go into the workaday real world again, half ashamed of the tears that we have shed over what was after all a play. The cross of Christ might exert some moral influence upon us when we thought that it was intended for something far profounder than the exertion of a moral influence upon us. But the moment we discover that after all it was but an exhibition and that Christ after all did not really do anything upon the cross that was absolutely necessary for our soul's salvation, then even that moral influence tends to disappear.

The true moral influence of the cross of Christ really comes, in other words, only when we see that the moral influence theory regarding it is false; it comes only when we see that on the cross Christ truly bore the penalty of our sins and buried it forever in the depths of the sea. He loves little to whom little is forgiven. If the sin for which we are forgiven is merely the light, easily forgiven thing that the advocates of the moral-influence theory of the atonement think it is, then no great spring of gratitude will well up in our souls toward Him who has caused us to be forgiven; but if it is the profound and deadly thing that the advocates of the substitutionary view of the atonement think it is, then all our lives will be one song of gratitude to Him who loved us and gave Himself for us upon the accursed tree.

From every point of view, therefore, the question with which we are now dealing is the most momentous question that could possibly be conceived. Did Christ die on the cross merely to influence us to holy and sacrificial living? Did He die on the cross merely to exhibit the necessity of some deterrent against sin in the interests of an orderly world, or did He die on the cross in order to pay the penalty of our sin and make us right with the holy God?

Which of these three views is right? That is the question which we shall seek to answer by an examination of the Word of God.

At the beginning of the examination there is one fact which stares us in the face. It has sometimes been strangely neglected. It is the fact of the enormous emphasis which the Bible lays upon the death of Christ.

Have you ever stopped to consider how strange that emphasis is? In the case of other great men, it is the birth that is celebrated and not the death. Washington's birthday is celebrated by a grateful American people on the twenty-second day of February, but who remembers on what day of the year it was that Washington died? Who ever thought of making the day of his death into a national holiday?

Well, there are some men whose death might indeed be celebrated by a national holiday, but they are not good men like George Washington; they are, on the contrary, men whose taking off was a blessing to their people. It would be a small compliment to the father of his country if we celebrated with national rejoicing the day when he was taken from us. Instead of that, we celebrate his birth. Yet in the case of Jesus it is the death and not the birth that we chiefly commemorate in the Christian church.

I do not mean that it is wrong for us to commemorate the birth of Jesus. We have just celebrated Christmas, and it is right for us so to do. Happy at this Christmas season through which we have just passed have been those to whom it has not been just a time of worldly festivity but a time of commemoration of the coming of our blessed Saviour into this world. Happy have been those men and women and little children who have heard, underlying all their Christmas joys, and have heard in simple and childlike faith, the sweet story that is told us in Matthew and Luke. Happy have been those celebrants of Christmas to whom the angels have brought again, in the reading of the Word of God, their good tidings of great joy.

Yes, I say, thank God for the Christmas season; thank God for the softening that it brings to stony hearts; thank God for the recognition that it brings for the little children whom Jesus took into His arms; thank God even for the strange, sweet sadness that it brings to us together with its joys, as we think of the loved ones who are gone. Yes, it is well that we should celebrate the Christmas season; and may God ever give us a childlike heart that we may celebrate it aright.

But after all, my friends, it is not Christmas that is the greatest anniversary in the Christian church. It is not the birth of Jesus that the church chiefly celebrates, but the death.

Did you know that long centuries went by in the history of the church before there is any record of the celebration of Christmas? Jesus was born in the days of Herod the King – that is, at some time before 4 B.C., when Herod died. Not till centuries later do we find evidence that the church celebrated any anniversary regarded as the anniversary of His birth.

Well, then, if that is so with regard to the commemoration of Jesus' birth, how is it with regard to the commemoration of His death? Was the commemoration of that also so long postponed? Well, listen to what is said on that subject by the Apostle Paul. 'For as often as ye eat this bread,' he says, 'and drink this cup, ye do shew the Lord's death till he come.' That was written only about twenty-five years after the death of Christ and after the founding of the church in Jerusalem. Even in those early days the death of Christ was commemorated by the church in the most solemn service in which it engaged – namely, in the celebration of the Lord's Supper.

203

Indeed that commemoration of the death of Christ was definitely provided for by Jesus Himself. 'This cup is the New Testament in my blood,' said Jesus: 'this do ye, as oft as ye drink it, in remembrance of me.' In those words of institution of the Lord's Supper, Jesus carefully provided that His church should commemorate His death.

Thus the Bible makes no definite provision for the commemoration of the birth of Jesus, but provides in the most definite and solemn way for the commemoration of His death.

What is the reason for that contrast, which at first sight might seem to be very strange? I think the answer is fairly clear. The birth of Jesus was important not in itself but because it made possible His death. Jesus came into this world to die, and it is to His death that the sinner turns when He seeks salvation for his soul. Truly the familiar hymn is right when it says about the cross of Christ:

> *All the light of sacred story*
> *Gathers round its head sublime.*

The whole Bible centres in the story of the death of Christ. The Old Testament looks forward to it; the New Testament looks back upon it; and the truly Biblical preacher of the gospel says always with Paul: 'I determined to know nothing among you, save Jesus Christ and him crucified.'

I ask you, then, which of the theories of the atonement suits this supreme emphasis which the Bible puts upon the cross.

Does the moral-influence theory suit it? I think not, my friends. If Jesus died on the cross merely to give us a good example of self-sacrifice or merely to exhibit, without underlying necessity, the love of God, then the Bible does seem strangely overwrought in the way in which it speaks of the death of Christ. Then indeed all the talk in the Bible about the blood of Christ and the blood of the sacrificial victims that were prophecies of Him becomes just about as distasteful as so many modern men hold it to be. Some very much greater significance must be attributed to the death of Christ than a mere hallowing of some universal law of self-sacrifice or a mere pedagogic exhibition of God's love, if we are to explain the way in which the Bible makes everything to centre in the event that took place on Calvary.

The case is not essentially different when we consider the governmental theory. It is true, the governmental theory does seek, as over against the moral-influence theory, to do justice to the emphasis which the Bible places just on the death of Christ. It regards the tragic horror of the cross not as merely incidental to the meaning of what Christ did but as essential to it. It regards that tragic horror as being the thing that shocks sinners out of their complacency and makes them recognise the seriousness of sin. Hence it seeks to show why just the death of Christ and not some other exhibition of self-sacrificing love was necessary.

But, after all, what a short way such considerations go towards explaining the Biblical emphasis on the cross of Christ! The truth is that there is just one real explanation of such emphasis. It is found in the fact that Christ on the cross did something absolutely necessary if we sinners are to be forgiven by a righteous God. Once recognise the enormous barrier which sin sets up between the offender and his God, once recognise the fact that that barrier is rooted not merely in the sinner's mind but in the eternal justice of God, and then once recognise that the cross, as the full payment of the penalty of sin, has broken down the barrier and made the sinner right with God – once recognise these things and then only will you understand the strange pre-eminence which the Bible attributes to the cross of Christ.

Thus even the mere prominence of the death of Christ

in the Bible, to say nothing of what the Bible says about the death of Christ in detail, is a mighty argument against all minimising theories of the significance of the death of Christ and a mighty argument in favour of the view that Christ on the cross really died in our stead, paying the dread penalty of our sin, that He might present us, saved by grace, before the throne.

In presenting what the Bible says in detail about the death of Christ, I want to speak first of all of those passages where Christ's death upon the cross is represented as a ransom, then about those passages where it is spoken of as a sacrifice, then about those passages where, without the use of either of these representations, its substitutionary or representative character is plainly brought out.

The first passage that we shall speak of, next Sunday afternoon, is that great passage in the tenth chapter of the Gospel according to Mark where our Lord says that the Son of Man came to give His life a ransom for many.

On this last Sunday of the old year, I just want to say to you who have been listening in on these Sunday afternoons how much encouraged I have been by your interest and by your Christian fellowship. I trust that you have had a very joyous Christmas and I trust that the new year which is so soon to begin may be to you a very blessed year under the mercy of God.

THE PSALMS OF LIFE

MOS

g\

Jerer

Davi

" Jesus wept "